To Mattie, I [illegible] more! [illegible]

Leviathan

The Bible's Darkest Metaphor

R. L. Nelson

Revealing the Missing Link to Comprehend Revelation

ISBN: 978-0-692-06332-3

ISBN: 978-0-595-46137-0

By Richard Lee

Table of Contents

Acknowledgments

Throughout the centuries, brilliant dedicated Christians searched scriptures hoping to unveil the mysteries of Revelation through eschatology. No matter how clever, intense, or how much belief that Revelation could be understood, the mysteries would hold until the latter days and this would only take place through the will of God.

Before setting the foundation of this book, I realized if these last biblical mysteries were to be revealed it would include the work of others. I believe some were on a right path. However, others were not. Listening to those that have a keen interest in prophecy often opened my eyes. This set my research in new directions and produced new scriptural connections. I especially love those that have challenged me and I would like to add that this book is not of private interpretation. Included is the Spirit of God, along with many others seeking the truth of biblical metaphors.

The Thomas Nelson NKJV, copyright 1988, has been my main tool of reference, even though the English structure does not line with todays configuration. I fully embrace the translators that enhanced the translations with added words (interpolations) that are not in the original Hebrew or Greek. These words give reverence, importance and significance. Therefore, I have copied word for word as they were written.

I thank my mother, Elizabeth, for the encouragement and guidance and to be explicit when writing a book like this. I especially would like to compliment my wife. Without her patience, this book would have never been written.

The Unger's Bible Dictionary, the Stone Edition Tanach and the Strong's Exhaustive Concordance of the Bible have been used in researching Leviathan.

This book has been revised to produce a more comprehensive study of this elusive metaphor taken from "Understanding Leviathan – The Key to the apostle John's "The Revelation," copyright 2008, published in 2010, under the pen name of Richard Lee.

Preface

The perception of Leviathan is based on an accumulation of scripture. This metaphorical fire breathing dragon first comes to us through the Book of Job. Other books of the Bible help shed light on how to convert this powerful metaphor into something that is real, literal and comprehensible. With extensive research Leviathan changes from a dragon with seven heads and ten horns, into a collection of kings and kingdoms. Researching this incredible metaphor lets Revelation give up its greatest mystery and conjecture is then replaced by a foundation. Its message sounds absurd, much like a dark fairytale. Yet, scripture confirms it. Through study, awareness is heightened. This mysterious metaphor spans the entire Bible. It is Leviathan, the missing link that brings Revelation to a new level of comprehension.

Throughout the ages the apostle John's mysterious book has never been fully explained. Today, new light now comes to biblical metaphors that have laid dormant for ages with little explanation. With examining and scrutinizing Leviathan's heads and horns, new information is acquired.

Along with Satan, God used this metaphorical seven-headed ten-horned beast to not only test the loyalty of his angels, but also his chosen ones. In the last days, Gentiles will also be tested. The end times becomes frightening as Leviathan's shadow begins to envelope the world. Our Lord explains why his saints will have to go through a tribulation of unmatched horror, as mankind will experience a time of trouble that has never been or will ever be again. With the comprehension of this dark dragon, as described in the Book of Job, our Lord will gain tremendous credibility, not only with today's believers, but also with many that have doubted Christianity.

Besides Leviathan, another metaphor will be viewed. This is Mystery Babylon, a great city symbolized by a harlot, a whore that sells herself off to the world. She receives her power and control through trade and eventually reigns over all kings and kingdoms. At her zenith, she will not see the coming of her imminent destruction. With information collected from Revelation's seventeenth and eighteenth chapters, the harlot strikingly parallels only one great city that today controls world trade.

She is rich and all nations will partake in her abominations. Trade is the cohesion of peace, the unification of this planet. This is why Osama Bin Laden destroyed the World Trade Center's Buildings. Today, there is a great city that controls world trade and also, it is targeted by terrorist. Their goal is to detonate a nuclear bomb and finish what they believe Allah asked them to do; destroy New York City and bring the world to its knees. By God's will, Leviathan's ten horns, which represent kings, will be called upon to destroy this great trade city. This will collapse world trade and then usher in the apocalypse. An ancient kingdom is prophesied to return, only to rise beyond any other and dominate the world. This comes through a spirit of evil. It will be intertwined with a false prophet and the power of Satan. With its rise, New York City will become consumed in a ball of fire.

Revelation's fourteenth chapter will give those that study prophecy, new insight. As it places events in their chronological order. Intrigue increases as a second angel proclaims the harlot's destruction. This will take place only after the gospel has been given to all dialects. It will separate Ancient Babylon from the apostle John's Mystery Babylon. After this, a third angel proclaims to everyone on earth that they will have a choice. Join with the beast and curse the one true God or die. Shortly, your faith and life will be challenged by a biblical metaphor. That being a powerful great fiery red dragon named Leviathan.

My mission is not to scare you, but to prepare you to what is to come.

"Enter by the narrow gate; for wide is the gate and broad is the way that leads to destruction, and there are many who go in by it. V14 Because narrow is the gate and difficult is the way which leads to life, and there are few who find it"

(Matthew 7:13-14).

Pieces of the Puzzle

Upon the completion of this book I would like you to return to these next images. I believe then you will fully understand the graphics and verses.

Leviathan
power, pride and evil

Revelation 14:6-7

"Then I saw another angel flying in the midst of heaven, having the everlasting gospel to preach to those who dwell on the earth - to every nation, tribe, tongue, and people - saying with a loud voice, "Fear God and give glory to Him, for the hour of His judgment has come; and worship Him who made heaven and earth, the sea and springs of water."

Matthew 24:14

"And this gospel of the kingdom will be preached in all the world as a witness to all the nations, and then the end will come."

Revelation 17:18
"And the woman whom you saw is that great city which reigns over the kings of the earth"

Revelation 17:16

"And the ten horns which you saw on the beast, these will hate the harlot, make her desolate and naked, eat her flesh and burn her with fire."

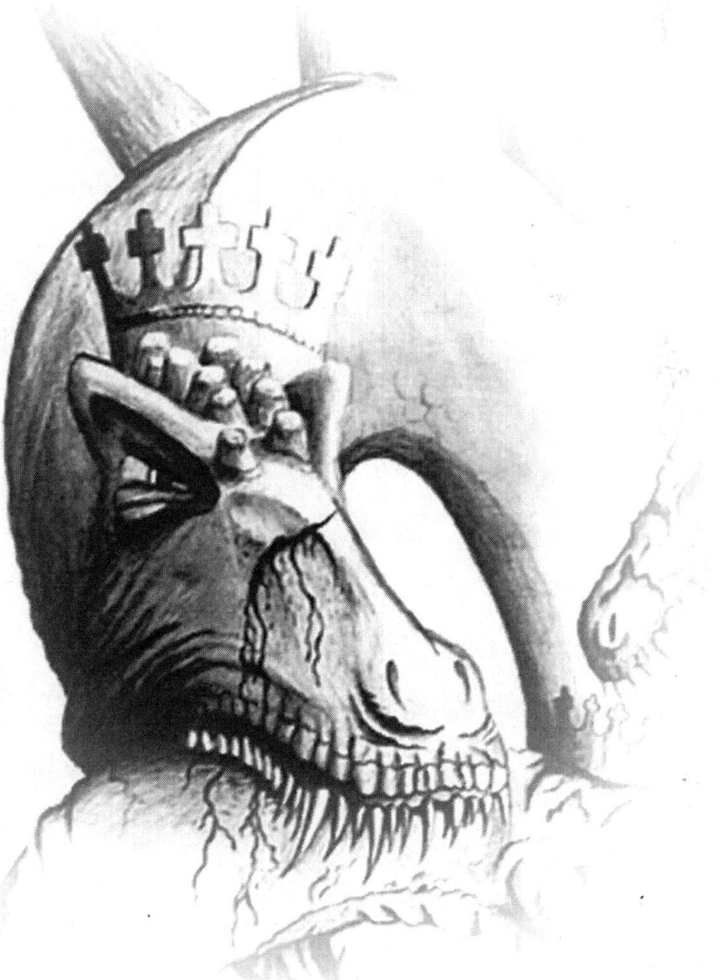

Then the end will come

Chapter 1

Tradition

It was terribly hot as I sat in my pew observing women fanning themselves. I don't believe air conditioning was yet invented, at least not for my church. Being at the age of eight, it was hard for me trying to listen to a man delivering his message with constant interruptions as babies screamed, hiccupped and burped nearby. I slowly withdrew as my mind began to wander. As I glanced down at the black book that laid on my lap, the surrounding noises slowly faded. I then proceeded to the last book in the Bible, Revelation. At that time of life I was consumed by dinosaurs, so I continued to my favorite verse lying in the thirteenth chapter. I quickly focused on the first verse and began to read as my mind exploded, visualizing a fierce beast rising up out of the sea; what a beast! This creature had seven heads and ten horns. I leaned over and gave my mother a slight nudge and whispered, "Is this a dinosaur?" Despairingly, all she did was to shrug her shoulders. With the completion of the sermon, relief came.

My mother drove on as I watched my church disappear from sight; this was my chance. I resumed my conversation with her about this great sea beast, trying to get an intelligent answer to satisfy my curiosity. What a letdown. Once again her shoulders rose, giving me her final answer as I sunk down in my seat.

Years passed, yet no one could help. In my teens I became consumed or you could say obsessed with this beast from the sea. Then one day I discovered a very unusual fire breathing dragon that no man could kill. Could this be real? After reading Job, Chapters 40 and 41, another mystery flourished without a satisfactory answer. What is the behemoth along with this great fire-breathing beast, Leviathan? Give me a break! Why in the world would there be a fire-breathing dragon inserted in the divinest of books, the Bible? After a few years, I became a professional photographer and was in an ideal position to ask many in the clergy about the subject relating to this dragon. Surprisingly, some did not know the name Leviathan even existed. What a disappointment! I continued to chase this beast into other books of the Bible, only to add confusion on top of confusion. The more questions that were asked, the more the answers were filled in by conjecture. Many times there was no scriptural foundation offered. In fact, many informed me that it was futile, that no man could unveil this mystery. Only God could. Then awareness crept in. This has been taught throughout the centuries as it removed many from proceeding any further. It also benefited a traditional way of viewing biblical mysteries, by avoiding them.

From within my church I began to wonder if I had the plague. Many would stare in disgust; too absurd! Traditionally, it has been the gospel that was taken seriously and why would anyone in their right mind want to study Revelation. What difference does it make? None realized the importance of connecting Job's Leviathan to the sea beast of Revelation. I agree about the importance of the gospel. Without Jesus, God's gift to the world, it would be useless to write this book. I often return to a very important question: what about the last twenty two chapters in the Bible given to us by our Lord Jesus, and a blessing that is bestowed on those who would eventually comprehend the book?

For years, I have been assured by godly men, many with honest intentions, that the book of Revelation could not be understood by human thought and believe it is so spiritual only God and his angels were to understand these writings. When the apostle John's book is addressed, many become irritated and feel intimidated. They quickly turn and walk away and by doing so the problem becomes apparent. A foundation is lacking and there is little quest for the mystery. Along with contradictions and conjecture, there has been a total lack of biblical knowledge, especially in the world of eschatology, scripture relating to the end days. Either for being inquisitive or for other reasons, I could not accept a view that no human could ever understand the last book of the Bible. Thankfully, the more I connected scripture the more my drive increased and motivated me to advance in my research. As my studies progressed other paths became apparent to unraveling its message. Gradually, a premise of what Revelation projected began to set in.

In Revelation, Chapter 10, an angel instructs John not to write certain things that will take place, mentioned in the uttering of the seven thunders. For a reason only God knows, he did not want us to understand certain future events. What does this tell us? The rest of the mysteries that John was shown are to be known, eventually, at the time of the end. His book of metaphors will be unveiled in the latter days, only to those that give an effort to comprehend.

"Blessed is he who reads and those who hear the words of this prophecy, and keep those things which are written in it; for the time is near" (Rev. 1:3).

The word "hear" means to understand what is being said. This is why they are called "blessed." The ones who hear have not turned their backs to John's prophetic book given to us from the one who is the spirit of prophecy, Jesus. Generations of seekers have been convinced that there is truth in the bible's last book. At the very end, some of the true believers will comprehend the darkest metaphor, Leviathan.

In the year 1651, Thomas Hobbes, a prominent English philosopher, mathematician and theorist, accepted by some as being versed in biblical scripture was the first to write an essay on Leviathan. He declared this fire-breathing dragon as a righteous powerful creature, representing the Commonwealth. Hobbes used this biblical metaphor to his own political advantage, not understanding that God created this powerful beast instilled with evil. It will eventually be terminated, as it tries to flee from the last great war that mankind will partake in. The point of this: many continue to take Hobbes as being a man that had great biblical knowledge. I believe there has been no other person on earth that has obscured the name of Leviathan more than Thomas Hobbes. Yet, this has not erased his error. Throughout the centuries his teachings have been handed down and accepted, especially in the academic arena and mainly without any form of biblical study. Hobbes has become a tradition to those that study economic philosophy and yet no one has a clue to the true meaning of this biblical metaphor.

Tradition can blind us to the point that no other truths can be inserted. New thoughts or ideas cannot be entertained because they do not follow the mainstream of what has been taught. Pride and tradition can run hand and hand. I have even heard it said, "My parents and even my grandparents believed this way, and I'm sure they weren't wrong." Many know and hold on to their own doctrines, yet they cannot tell you much of what has been written in the Bible or how it relates to their lives. Knowledge is often rejected because of tradition. Even apostle Paul embraced tradition.

"And I advanced in Judaism beyond many of my contemporaries in my own nation, being more exceedingly zealous for the traditions of my fathers" (Gal. 1:14).

Paul did his job well! He was exceedingly zealous and blinded by the tradition of his forefathers and later blinded by God. Blinded to see again, only after he was given new light. Paul had to lay down his past in order to possess a new spirit, to carry out the will of God. Because God gave him additional grace, scales were removed from his eyes and for the first time he could see through his forefather's traditions and realize that Jesus is truly the Son of God.

Tradition is often cherished more than spiritual knowledge. Like Paul, one can be blinded from the truth without ever understanding why. Stephen was a man of God and broke from the traditional Jewish Sanhedrin law and was stoned to death for doing so. As were many others, because of the knowledge they found in the gospel of the Lord and the Torah. The adherents of the old covenant were not easily persuaded to acknowledge this man Jesus. Their leaders were blinded by the law and would not allow their hearts to open to the Holy Spirit. Tradition kept God's word alive, but it also suppressed truth. Many were martyred having the understanding of God's will, having opened their hearts to Jesus.

Christians often look down on others because of religious differences. This has caused wars and deaths of millions. We are informed that God is not the author of confusion, so where does the finger point?

Although we have to understand that God tells us that there is a time for war, a time to kill (Eccl. 3.3). Otherwise, there would be no freedom of religion. Many warlords have led man against man and had nothing to do with the true God of heaven. In fact, some believed they were a god.

Traditionally, Protestants have viewed the Roman Catholic Church as the harlot represented in the seventeenth and eighteenth chapter of Revelation. They believe this church is corrupted and leads the world to destruction. Interestingly, the Roman Catholic Church has viewed Protestants as the harlot, the ones that left the mother church. They are eternally lost unless they return to Catholicism. I believe neither quite have it right. As it has been, tradition has played a part on both sides and kept the true picture from being known.

With an increase in biblical knowledge, more are realizing that the coming of our Lord is very close. For the first time in almost two thousand years scripture now parallels current events. Understanding the Revelation of Jesus Christ gives us, for the first time, enough information between Daniel, Jeremiah, Isaiah, Job, Psalm and the book of Revelation to comprehend the mystery of Leviathan and that of the harlot, Mystery Babylon, the great city. We are not to know the day or the hour when the Lord returns. Only God knows this! What we are to know is that the mystery of Revelation will be revealed.

Chapter 2

A Blessing

Before setting a premise, an entire overview has to be studied and then a presentation can be offered. If a dog is to be examined, don't concentrate on the flea. What is the overall foundation of Revelation? Prepare to persevere to the end and hold on to your eternal crown, because most true believers will eventually lose their heads over their testimony of Jesus and the true God.

Most of us spent the earlier part of our lives being sheltered by the love of our parents or guardians, driving us to success, along with walking the straight and narrow. Just about every Christian that I know proclaim they believe in a God of love; one that protects and never leaves you, no matter what! Can it be this simple, just trusting in a living and loving God without being fed to wolves? Would God allow any that serve him to be tormented or to be cast into the hands of those that are evil or to be stripped of this earthly life? Many pastors slide their doctrines in between the pages of Revelation so that their congregations refrain from covering their children ears. Otherwise, they would quickly drag them from their pews, never to return again. Their sermons continually carry the theme of tranquility.

The big question: is the one of authority giving the right interpretation and possibly frightened about losing their entire congregation?

What kind of God do you believe in? I hear many times, "I know that I'm saved, so reading Revelation doesn't really interest me." I believe those who think this way do not understand the message that is given in the last book of the Bible.

Why is there a blessing in Revelation 1:3? Is there a warning to believers that just professing the Lord's name guarantees you an eternal crown? In fact, one third of God's angels fell from his grace and were deceived by the great red dragon, intertwined with another great dragon, Satan. They were cast from heaven down to earth and will eventually land in hell because of it.

In the twentieth century approximately six million Jews were exterminated which became known as the holocaust. These were God's chosen ones. They rejected his will and turned their backs on him. Isaiah, Chapter 66, explains why God came against his people.

Did the holocaust happen because the Jews were stiff necked and turned away from truth? Did God allow Hitler, a white supremacist, who wanted to exterminate the Jews just to create a purely German nation? Those of Jewish blood became destined to destruction (2 Chr. 30:8). Could God have stopped or prevented this? Does he allow tyrants to challenge his believers? Ones that will let you live, if only you reject God or Jesus? If so, they have snatched their souls. Without testing a proclaimed believer, would there be glory to him that has created us?

"Blessed is he who reads and those who hear the words of this prophecy, and keep those things which are written in it; for the time is near" (Rev. 1:3).

"It was granted to him to make war with the saints and to overcome them. And authority was given him over every tribe, tongue, and nation. V8 All who dwell on the earth will worship him, whose names have not been written in the Book of Life of the Lamb slain from the foundation of the world" (Rev. 13:7-8).

"He shall speak *pompous* words against the Most High, Shall persecute the saints of the Most High, And shall intend to change times and law. Then *the saints* shall be given into his hand For a time and times and half a time" (Dan. 7:25).

The great tribulation will be the worst of times for everyone on earth. Man and Satan's wrath will destroy this world, and if not for the intervention of God, even his elect (Isa. 45:4) would be lost (Matt. 24:21-22).

In the fifth seal there are souls under the altar that have been slain for the word of God and the testimony of Jesus. They cry out to God, wondering when he will stop the slaughter of their brethren.

The word "blessed" can take on many different interpretations. Some view the meaning as contented, cheerful or happy. Others connect it to tribulation as Revelation 14:13 explains: "Blessed are the dead that die in the Lord from now on." This passage is connected to the great tribulation and the mark of the beast. These are true believers, beheaded for the testimony of Jesus and the true God (Rev. 20:4-6).

Twenty two chapters will eventually give up the mystery that God has hidden from us. Only at the time of the end will this prophetic book of confusing metaphors be understood. Jesus delivered this revelation to the apostle John in 96 AD. This is when he wrote Revelation, but his book would not be understood until the very last of days, just before the Lords' return. Without John's information that connects many sectors of the Bible, believers would be left in a void, held back from very important chronological events that have to take place. With the rebirth of Israel, events begin to align with latter-day prophecy. With the unveiling of Revelation, our Lord will then be treasured by many that just before had questioned his authenticity. He will receive recognition and creditability that none other could achieve and will be held as the Lord of Lords, as the true spirit of prophecy and the true Messiah.

Today, many ask for proof and demand, "Show us a sign!" Besides faith, is there any substance, especially in the realm of prophecy that could lead one to Christianity? The answer: absolutely! I fully believe those who comprehend Revelation understand that this Leviathan metaphor, the missing link, has been completely passed over and over since the time the name was written. Its symbolism has everything to do with opening our eyes to what lies in store for the future of our country, along with the great city of trade and the future of the godly and ungodly. With the mystery removed, fear will enter those that previously viewed the end days as a type of tranquility; no pain, no tribulation as each true believer floats up to the clouds to meet our savior.

In Revelation's seven seals, the first through the fourth are considered to be "The Apocalypse of the Four Horsemen" also known as "The Great Tribulation." The fifth seal is an extension of this upcoming horror. This draws to an end when God stops the tremendous slaughter of his saints, but only when the number is fulfilled. The killing of the Christian and Jew slows to a trickle as God's wrath begins with the ones that have killed his believers.

"Then I heard a voice from heaven saying to me, "Write: Blessed *are* the dead who die in the Lord from now on." "Yes," says the Spirit, "that they must rest from their labors, and their works follow them." (Rev. 14:13).

I would like to comment on the fourteenth chapter. There is no other sector that gives a more transparent picture relating to the end of time. In chronological order three angels proclaim:

- The gospel will be given to all nations, peoples, tongues and tribes, all dialects. Then the end begins. Judgment comes upon mankind.

- Mystery Babylon, the great city is then destroyed. This is a city that controls the trade of the world. Peace is then removed from the earth.

- The mark of the beast now enters with the beginning of the apocalypse, the great tribulation. Christians will then be killed (beheaded) as they defend and profess their faith, proving themselves worthy.

Only after the great city is destroyed will believers in Christ be faced with an option. They must join the dark side or stay in the light. Lose your head but not your soul. To endure in faith is the ultimate goal. Those who die in the name of the Lord from there on are called "blessed." Could this be the blessing that at the time of the great tribulation one could prove their faith by sacrificing their life to the evil beast in the name of Jesus? Matthew 24:13 informs the believer; "But he who endures to the end shall be saved." With this, we also see suffering. The beast with the mark (Rev. 14:11) is the same beast in Revelation 13:11–18. The Jewish Tanach comments on Isaiah 57:1–2. He addressed the wicked people of his generation and explains that at a time when righteous people are not respected they may die so that they should not witness the evil that is about to come upon the world. They are far better off dead than being underfoot of these evil rulers. If you have to trade your soul for an earthly life, and a short earthly life, would it be worth it? Be worthy and endure. I don't believe in killing one's self, but I have not been in a situation that could be that dire.

"We are bound to thank God always for you, brethren, as it is fitting, because your faith grows exceedingly, and the love of every one of you all abounds toward each other, V4 so that we ourselves boast of you among the churches of God for your patience and faith in all your persecutions and tribulations that you endure, V5 which is manifest evidence of the righteous judgment of God, that you may be counted worthy of the kingdom of God, for which you also suffer; V6 since it is a righteous thing with God to repay with tribulation those who trouble you, V7 and to give you who are troubled rest with us when the Lord Jesus is revealed from heaven with His mighty angels" (2 Thess. 1:3–7).

"Let no one deceive you by any means; for that Day will not come unless the falling away comes first, and the man of sin is revealed, the son of perdition, V4 who opposes and exalts himself above all that is called God or that is worshiped, so that he sits as God in the temple of God, showing himself that he is God" (2 Thess. 2:3–4).

There is too much preaching that Jesus could appear right at this moment. Not according to scripture! Our Lord will not appear today because of this information. Could Christ return tomorrow, next week, or next year? Not until this prophecy unfolds!

Let's put this in perspective. Paul is writing to the Thessalonians, explaining that there is evidence for them to be counted worthy through enduring in their tribulations. Then he jumps to the future, to the last days. We see the great apostasy, a massive falling away from God's truth. This takes place when the man of perdition reveals himself with all the destruction and killing of the prophets and saints. Shortly after this, all nations of the world will be gathered to fight God's chosen, in the land of Israel. Christ eventually comes with his legions of angels to destroy the wicked and punish all nations that went against Israel. Along with the ones that have divided her land. Jesus will return on the last trumpet, which is in the seventh and last seal. There are seven trumpets and the Lord will return on the very last one.

All around me I hear many say that things are not right and believe the world is coming to an end and this is part of the equation of why the interest in prophecy. Sorry to say there has been a spike in sensationalism, especially with the book of Revelation. Throughout the last several decades I am often asked about current events and are they related to Revelation? Nowhere in the Bible are we informed about the Civil War, Hiroshima, walking on the moon, WW II, severe hurricanes, tornadoes and many other extreme events. We are informed that complexity, wars and rumors of wars, pestilence and earthquakes, along with lawlessness will abound. Everything revolves around the State of Israel and someday the world will be drawn to Armageddon, the last great war as mankind will attempt to exterminate the Jew.

Revelation's twelfth chapter begins with a woman clothed with the sun, with the moon under her feet and on her head lays a garland of twelve stars. She was with child and cried out as she gave birth. Here we see the woman Israel adorned with twelve stars, her twelve tribes giving birth to Jesus. Leviathan's tail drew one third of the heavenly angels to earth, they were deceived by Satan. The devil has been cast down to earth and later begins his quest to destroy Israel and to kill God's only son.

"The Revelation 12 Sign" gives an interpretation that seems to connect to astrology and to a rapture of the church. From point to point, opinions (conjecture) are constantly introduced and this leads those into a realm that has nothing to do with the true sense of what was meant. In 2012 many believed in a Mayan prophecy relating to the destruction of the world. The ones that considered this belief had little or no instruction in the Bible, especially in the book of Revelation. Many have put their faith in a man named Nostradamus in which his first writings appeared in 1555. Many today still embrace his predictions. It is claimed that one of these pointed to the burning of New York City in the year 1999. Without a doubt he was a false prophet. A true prophet is never wrong! Some claimed there was a spiritual connection to the 2017 eclipse. It was impressive, but most do not realize that there have been hundreds of these events that have been recorded over the last five thousand years. I often hear giants will again roam the earth, relating to Genesis 6. This is not the message given in Matthew 24:37-39. When man does not look for the return of our Lord, this is when he comes, as a thief in the night. As in the days of Noah, there will be eating, drinking, marrying and giving in marriage and no worry about the Lord's return. At the time of the end the world will not be prepared. Lately, there have been many hurricanes and many proclaim this is part of the "Signs and Wonders" described in Luke 21 and Matthew 24. These natural events do not relate to the context of these two authors but rather we see false prophets creating signs and wonders. Also, at the very end, at the time of God's wrath, heavenly events connect to the sun, moon and stars. This pertains to the sixth and seventh seals. This is at the very end and does not take place until the great tribulation has ended.

There have been many soothsayers that claimed to know the future, mostly for their own gain. My faith is in the Holy Scripture, not in the teachings of other cultures, babbling from false teachers, particularly the ones that have not believed in Jesus or the true Hebrew God. As we see in Revelation, blessed are those who have an eye and ear, to understand this last book of the Bible, for the time is ripe. This knowledge could keep many from falling into a future false religion that will condemn their souls. Knowing the truth and what to expect will reinforce one's faith. The information given by Revelation is a blessing!

Some believe Revelation points to our current world government that will eventually force everyone to receive an inserted electronic chip, either in the forehead or right hand. The chip will record every move and transaction. If any do not conform to this, none will be able to buy or sell as we are informed in Revelation's thirteenth chapter. Another view will be presented and show that this current government is not the one to fear, another will follow. This pertains to a false prophet and his religion and connects to Satan. At that time, many will fall from the true faith, along with losing their souls.

Think about the United States of America. Is there a connection to Revelation? Do you believe our economic or foreign policies are on the right track? Are you happy, frustrated or ambivalent toward them? Do you believe we are slowly destroying this nation by selling ourselves off to the world? Would God be happy with the direction we have taken, especially trying to pacify countries through trade, the ones of hate that want to destroy us? Are you positive that you don't belong to the harlot, Mystery Babylon, the great city of Revelation? Without studying prophecy and setting a premise, you cannot say! Is Rome the kingdom that is prophesied to return in the latter days? Again, if you don't research and study prophetic scripture you cannot have a concrete answer, only conjecture, only a guess. If you think your faith will not be challenged and believe this country has no part in biblical prophecy, please keep reading. Finally, if you do not understand the urgency to comprehend Leviathan, by the end of this book you will be able to fully grasp the most powerful, dangerous and dark metaphor entered in the Bible, for it will shortly affect your faith and life.

Have you ever heard "One word does not make a difference?" In the realm of eschatology one word can affect a premise and the interpretation can become flawed, leading one away from truth. To some, they could care less. To others who are trying to unlock the mysteries, one word can make all the difference, especially in regard to the mystery of the sea serpent Leviathan. A blessing is given to those who are in the spirit of prophecy, believing with all their heart and soul that the words of prophecy are true and the metaphorical symbolism is to be understood.

There is a disturbing side which bothers me. Many sit through sermons listening to words of prophecy, trusting the deliverer of that message is authoritative and versed in the subject. Myself, I have sat through classes and sermons that preached on the end days along with voices delivered from the audience, "That's right brother, that's right!" Are there reasons to challenge? Should bibles be opened and scripture researched in order to confirm the messenger? Are there any that have enough scriptural knowledge in the realm of eschatology (scripture relating to the last days) to tell what or who is right or wrong? The "blessing" in Revelation 1:3 relates to understanding the message of the revelation and the only way to obtain that knowledge is through research, to gather information in order to set a foundation. Then when one speaks on the subject, you can either accept or challenge.

I have read Revelation 1:3 many times and informed there would be a special blessing. I couldn't quite get it. Why a blessing? Was I going to receive a gift, a special blessing just by reading the book? That verse bothered me for years. Some shake their heads and proclaim that the apostle John was delirious or crazy when he wrote Revelation. Some blaspheme the book, completely denying the existence of any truth to his writing. Do they also receive a blessing for reading Revelation? Myself, I had absolutely no idea of all that would be given (Matthew 7:7-8). By understanding Leviathan, this seven-headed ten-horned sea beast, a treasure was given to me that is beyond any earthly treasure. This, without a doubt is a blessing! Let's study this next verse and see what information we can acquire.

"Blessed is he who reads and those who hear the words of this prophecy, and keep those things which are written in it; for the time is near" (Rev. 1:3).

In Greek, the word "*hear*" means to understand. Blessed is he who reads and those who understand this prophecy. In this context the one reading understands the words and delivers them to the one that hears. The one that has put an effort into trying to unravel the mystery and held a belief that truth has always existed in Revelation. This completely changes this thought of a "blessing." I believe one has to be in the spirit in order to obtain this blessing. The ones that scoff at John's book failed and did not keep those things which are written in it. Revelation 22:18–19, also warns not to add or remove words pertaining to the book. If any are not in spirit it would be impossible to understand these words of prophecy. It is only through persistence, believing and examining scripture, that one will confirm the message given and then be able to comprehend its true meaning. There has to be commitment in order to receive a blessing for understanding Revelation.

What is the meaning "for the time is near?" What are these last few words telling us? Understand, this was written around 96 AD, so how could anyone back then say "for the time is near?" We are looking at a little less than two thousand years ago when this was written. Could it be that John really was crazy? No, he was not even near delirious or crazy, but he was indwelled with a spirit and the truth of his vision would not be understood until the latter days. I believe he was given this verse with prophecy connected to it. It is significant that when the one who understands the words of Revelation also understands that "the time is near," (Rev. 1:3). Once John's metaphorical book is unveiled, mankind is at its end and the time is near to the returning of our Lord. The Gentile rule is about to end as God's judgment is about to begin. We are almost out of time.

Chapter 3

Establishing a Premise

John is the apostle that wrote Revelation. Some believe the book was written before 70 AD, before the destruction of the temple in Jerusalem. John was exiled to the island of Patmos by the order of the Roman Emperor Domitian and this happened in 96 AD. This is when he wrote Revelation. After studying the Book of Daniel and then applying it to Revelation, many do not realize that hundreds of years passed between the two prophets. Yet the substance of what was written lets vital information flow between their writings. When comparing these books, one can begin to establish a premise that will eventually reveal Leviathan. Without having the wisdom to connect other books of the Bible, the mystery of Leviathan would never be revealed.

"The Revelation of Jesus Christ, which God gave Him to show His servants—things which must shortly take place. And He sent and signified *it* by His angel to His servant John" (Rev.1:1)

His servants are to be shown things that will shortly take place. John gives greetings and addresses the seven churches, which sat in Asia

Minor. He then writes of his revelation delivered by an angel.

Revelation 1:19*,* John is told, "Write the things which you have seen, and the things which are, and the things which will take place after this." This verse gives a past, present and future. In the study of the seven churches our Lord pointed out the condition of each church, where they once stood, and the condition they were in at the time John wrote Revelation. Our Lord also gave these churches blessings and warnings. The word "caution" quickly creeps in. If you do not change your direction and repent soon; God will remove his angels, his lampstands. The first three chapters are devoted to the reverence of Jesus and God and address the seven churches past and present and attached conditions that have to be upheld. In the fourth chapter we leave the seven churches and enter into something that is not totally of this earth, but connected to heaven.

"After these things I looked, and behold, a door *standing* open in heaven. And the first voice which I heard *was* like a trumpet speaking with me, saying, "Come up here, and I will show you things which must take place after this" (Rev. 4:1).

John is now going to be shown "things that must take place after this," looking beyond the time of the seven churches. He is about to be shown a vision of the future. The word "shortly" is omitted from this verse, unlike Revelation 13:1. This took away the urgency to resolve Revelation, especially in John's life time when there would be no need to comprehend the entire book. Keep in mind Revelation was written around 96 AD. Babylon, Persia and Greece have already been destroyed. Jesus has been crucified, resurrected and ascended to heaven. A door has now been opened to heaven and John is shown future events that must take place. It is very important to understand that we are now looking into the future. This is why setting a premise is so important in the study of eschatology. John was shown the past state of the seven churches, the condition of the churches along with blessings and warnings at the time of John and after. This leads to the future of a spiritual and sinful world.

The veil is slowly lifting and many prophetic books of the Bible will then be viewed with new understanding. The Book of Daniel has been sealed from the time of Daniel. Revelation is not to be sealed because it brings us through the time of the end.

"But you, Daniel, shut up the words, and seal the book until the time of the end; many shall run to and fro, and knowledge shall increase" (Daniel 12:4).

Through study, I now realize Revelation has kept many chasing its mysteries. It is a book written about the past, present and future, especially relating to the latter days. Without the Book of Daniel or Revelation, none of us could be brought to this pinnacle. Understanding prophecy relates to the timing of our Lord's return. By combining both books, clues are given and an increase in transparency begins to abound as information begins to flow, which eventually removes this veil of secrecy. Only then can pieces of the prophetic puzzle be placed in their right order to give a true picture. I believe Revelation 1:3 is informing us that blessed are those who understand the writings of the book of Revelation also understands that the time is near. In other words, the time is short. *Prepare yourself for what is to come and understand your God.* Understand why you are about to go through a test of faith. Our time is short before both Antichrists show themselves and the saints will be delivered into their hands and killed. Once these writings are understood, we are almost out of time. The world will be judged and *judgment begins with the house of the Lord.*

Always keep in mind to how close the entire world is to receiving the gospel of the Lord, which triggers the beginning of the end. Even though the gospel is being spread throughout the globe, it amazes me how fast America has fallen from Christianity and at an ever increasing rate. As Islamic Sharia law begins to engulf the world, what used to be strong Christian nations now step back without a fight and allow this evil to enter their lands. It is ironic that many in the clergy have closed their lips, believing God will deliver them from tribulation. Publishers are also beginning to feel the pressures of Islam as many will not print material that displays their religion in a bad light. President Obama confirmed this by saying "The future does not belong to those that slander the prophet of Islam." You can print any kind of material about Islam, as long as it shows goodness and harmony. Then there is no worry about repercussion: Islam 1, Christians 0. We are not all brothers in Christ and slowly we back off from the challenges that face us.

Can You Lose What You Gained?

In the first chapters of Revelation, the message to the seven churches is an example of this. Your crown of salvation can be lost. If one does not endure, persevere, adhere to the message given to them, that person can lose it all. If a righteous man sins and follows the ways of the wicked and dies in that sin, all the good he has done is for nothing. His righteousness will not be remembered and he will be judged in sin (Ezek. 18:24–32). This scripture also gives another view. If anyone is in sin and turns to righteousness, that person will be given a crown of eternal salvation.

It is prophesied that in the latter days there will be a falling away from the true faith (2 Thess. 2:3). Again, the message of the Lord is to endure. Especially what is about to come upon the whole world, referring to the great tribulation. As the end nears there will be many false philosophies, faiths, christs and doctrines given by false teachers. Tribulation will face the latter day Christian and apparently with the prophecy of the apostasy (the falling away from the true faith) many will not persevere. This will come by backing away from the truth of the Bible and possibly converting to a false god or religion. The message: you can lose your spiritual crown of salvation or you can gain your crown of salvation. It is written many times in Revelation, "He who overcomes." The question: can you endure and hold on to the one and only true faith?

The more I study, the more I realize that there is no way out. As the second seal opens, we see not only peace taken from the earth but also we see a great sword that represents tremendous death that will fall upon mankind. I know many of us have been taught that if we are true believers we are not to partake in this great tribulation that is prophesied to come. I will express through scripture and not just conjecture, we will have to travel the same road to the cross as Christ.

There are those who believe we will war with Islam and win! Some believe in Islamic prophecy with Jesus returning with his mighty angels and helping the Mahdi (Islamic prophet) in conquering evil. Revelation portrays to everyone that grasps the book, that there is an urgency to understand. Until the Day of the Lord, Christians are going to go through a test, a hell that will separate the true from the false. Revelation warns us of this upcoming event and to not put ourselves into a false state of security and belong to a church of wishful thinking. If Christians believe they will be removed before the great tribulation, then the shock of the evil one that is to come will overtake them. Without comprehending the last book in the Bible, many will fall to this prophesied mark placed on their right hand or forehead, which will join them to a false religion. This will cause many that had endured in faith to lose their eternal and glorious crown. As time progresses in the great tribulation, there is a possibility that exceedingly strong Christians will begin to doubt their Lord. They will think that he has let them down and did not remove them from the greatest time of trouble that will eventually engulf this planet. Many will begin to trust in a prophetic doctrine that has no merit, offering a doctrine of deception that has been created by Satan.

Was Peter prepared when he denied Christ three times? Did he understand the message that the Lord was giving? Wasn't Christ going to deliver him from the hands of the Romans? Yet, he was given more than one opportunity when he turned and denied knowing Jesus. When that time comes to the latter-day Christian, they might not have that privilege of a second or third chance. We have to carry with us at all times the armor of God so we will not fail this final upcoming test. Understand, being "saved" does not mean you will be kept from tribulation. In fact, just the opposite! The ones who die in the name of the Lord will be called "blessed." Endure to the end because it's not going to be pretty!

Revelation is not a book of all doom and gloom. When the Lord returns, the light will brighten beyond imagination and will only be seen by those that overcome. They will share in a glory that most of the world will never know.

The blessing in Revelation 1:3 comes from understanding the will of God and he is not to be taken lightly. He is not just a friend but one that will eventually challenge your soul, to the option of losing it. For a short time Satan's offering will become very attractive. Don't buy into it. The next time you hear Revelation is no big deal, give it a little deeper thought.

The Curse

At one time I watched a prominent television evangelist give, what I thought was going to be an impressive presentation on Revelation's seven seals. The main subject was the four horses and their riders, representing the apocalypse, an event of unparalleled death that is prophesied to overtake the earth. These are the first four seals, beginning in Revelation's sixth chapter. After finishing the fourth seal the television station took a lengthy break for ads. As the presentation continued he then presented the sixth seal. What happened to the fifth seal and why was it never mentioned? The reason: if this man would have included what he omitted, his premise would have crumbled and put him into a world of paradox by leaving out the continued killing of the saints. This had to be done because of a doctrine that has been embraced for over a hundred years. In other words, this minister has removed words from Revelation. Prior to this, Islamic eschatology has injected a false amount of material that connects to Revelation. The Mahdi, the last of the twelve Imams (prophets), will fight alongside Jesus and clear a path for the return of Allah, which is Islam's supreme god. In addition to Revelation, the Mormons have also written their own versions of prophecy along with Nostradamus, Edgar Cayse and a large number of soothsayers giving doctrines that do not declare the facts. Their writings have to be scrutinized by the last book in the Bible, Revelation. Many have and many still try to inject scripture into the apostle John's book of deep metaphors, only to satisfy their own ears. Those that acknowledge scripture will come to a truth.

In the last chapter of Revelation there is a warning along with a curse. There is a promise to any that add or remove words of Jesus written in this book of prophecy.

"For I testify to everyone who hears the words of the prophecy of this book: If anyone adds to these things, God will add to him the plagues that are written in this book; V19 and if anyone takes away from the words of the book of this prophecy, God shall take away his part from the Book of Life, from the holy city, and *from* the things which are written in this book" (Rev. 22:18-19).

Jesus has given his believers an outline of the end days. Revelation should be read over and over and over, without the interference of any doctrine that changes the books direction. Then it is up to the reader to acknowledge John's words. If the foundation on what you stand begins to crumble, then let go of any pride and pray for the wisdom to comprehend. Can your constitution of belief be challenged by Revelation? There is no mention of a "taking up," a removal of Christians before the great tribulation. In fact, the fifth seal informs the reader that just the opposite will take place.

As I absorbed Revelation, I began to view it as a transparent box filled with the words of Jesus. Scripture is seen floating inside, being protected from any external source and was set there for all to view. Only the words that are contained within are to be interpreted and John gives warning to any that add or omit words that are written in this prophetic book of Jesus. If the premise of this book is altered in any way, a curse will come to those who try.

We can only interpret what lies in Revelation and may not remove or place doctrines or words in between its pages. Excessive martyrdom will carry on until God begins his wrath.

Chapter 4

Building a Foundation

Why is there so little known about this name Leviathan that exists in the Old Testament and why did God obscure the true meaning of this mystery? Did he fill in vacancies throughout the Bible just to add more words of unknown meaning, relating to this sea beast as read in Isaiah, Job, Psalm and Revelation? Could it be that this beast is mythological, an absurd fable that somehow became part of the Holy Scriptures? Or can we look in another direction, a mystery represented by a metaphor, a symbolism representing something that is real, of power, pride and evil?

Fire breathing dragons have shared many ancient cultural beliefs and still do. It is said the Babylonians carved a seven-headed beast on the gates to their city. Images of dragons have been carved into wood and stone and collected from around the world. Some signify power and others evil, many times both. The question: what do dragons have to do with the Bible? Are these fire-breathing beasts only a fable or is there any kind of truth attached to them? If we cannot believe one part of the Bible, why should we believe another? Biblical scholars have debated the subject. Some declare Leviathan to be a fire-breathing dragon that relates to some kind of dinosaur. Satan is also represented by a serpent or dragon. Others proclaim it to be a beast that lives in the sea that has not yet shown itself. Some view this sea beast as mythological and others see it as metaphorical; being symbolic, representing something real and meaningful.

Throughout the years I have conversed with believers in the Bible and Christ. Surprisingly, some did not know that the name Leviathan even existed. Others could not fathom this beast moving from one segment of the Bible into another. The main reason is that this beast's proper name of Leviathan is not mentioned in the New Testament, only in the Old. By now it can be understood why there has been so much misinterpretation, and this is only part of it. We now have entertainment, finance, food, energy, alongside a newly-found gas field in Israel, along with countless others that carry the name of Leviathan and of course the confusion of Thomas Hobbes and his followers. How can anyone arrive to the truth of this dark biblical metaphor?

I have attended many Bible classes that relate to the latter days. None were taught the same and there was no connection to this sea beast, with the exception of older bibles that included depictions of this creature rising up out of the sea as mentioned in the thirteenth chapter of Revelation. The comprehension expressing the importance and urgency did not exist, although a light is beginning to brighten. At the present there are ongoing discussions, realizing there is a missing link that would unravel Revelation's mysteries. Contrary to this, controversy is brewing within the frame work of Christianity. There is becoming a dismissal of the apostle John's Revelation, again brought on by lack of understanding, especially a book that no one could decipher. None would understand until the latter days. I believe it is time to keep the compass from spinning and focus in one direction, a missing link that will eventually unveil God's deepest secrets that lie in the apostle John's book of dark metaphors.

Isaiah 27:1 informs us that Leviathan lives in the sea. Is this the same sea beast as in Revelation 13:1, rising up out of the sea? What is the significance of its ten horns and seven heads? Does it have a body and tail? Are there other scriptures that might solve its identity? Let's begin to build a premise, a foundation so Leviathan can be viewed, not as mythological but rather metaphorical. Converting its symbolism to a literal view involves a large amount of scriptural investigation. God's most beautiful cherub became known to the world as a serpent or snake, representing one that is low, a spirit of evil. Satan, the serpent of old, will never rise to the esteem that he once held. Leviathan is no different. In the Book of Job, Leviathan is portrayed as a fire-breathing dragon. A power that mankind cannot deal with. It will be presented that Leviathan actually represents kings and kingdoms, along with power, pride and evil.

Revelation is a book of many segments and its clues must be rethought. They have been read but never fully understood. Only when these symbolic metaphors have been converted into a literal understanding are we able to lay the pieces of the puzzle in order to build a foundation. This will ultimately lead to a true understanding of how Leviathan represents not only history, but also latter-day prophecy. Let's begin to convert its symbolisms and look at them as representing something real, logical and comprehensible.

Taken from the NKJV. We now look at a symbol, a mountain or mountains. "Here is the mind which has wisdom: The seven heads are seven mountains on which the woman sits" (Rev. 17:9). This verse enlightens us that the heads represent mountains and are an important part in revealing Leviathan. So, what do "mountains" represent?

"Behold, I *am* against you, O destroying mountain, Who destroys all the earth," says the Lord. "And I will stretch out my hand against you, Roll you down from the rocks, And make you a burnt mountain" (Jer. 51:25).

God reveals that he is about to destroy the kingdom of Babylon. He will make her a burnt mountain, a burnt kingdom! There are other verses that show that a mountain is not always a literal mountain, but a symbol to represent a kingdom of great power (Isaiah 65:25, 66:20, Jeremiah 3:6, Daniel 2:35, 2:45, and Matthew 17:20). I believe if one has enough faith one can move a mountain, a kingdom. Daniel 2:45 informs us that a stone was cut out of a mountain without hands. When this is compared to other scripture, we then understand this cornerstone represents Jesus. He is the cornerstone, the foundation of God's eternal kingdom, cut from a mountain.

I am not writing to dismiss the New International Version. In the realm of eschatology, I personally have several issues with that version. We see in the NIV that the seven mountains of Revelation 17:9 are translated as "hills." Many interpret "hills" as relating to the "Seven Hills of Rome." This translation leads many to believe that Ancient Rome is the kingdom that is prophesied to return in the latter days to again conquer the world. This would include an evil pope leading the charge. It will be discussed why this interpretation is flawed.

In the seventh chapter of Daniel, we are informed that "beasts" represent kingdoms and their kings are included. This is a very important clue leading you to how to count the number of a beast, for it is a number of a man, Rev. 13:18. This also connects to seven kings (men) and then focusing on the last two kings that are of immense evil, Rev. 17:10. Revelation 17:11 is also part of the equation, informing us that there are eight beasts (kingdoms) and once Leviathan is assembled with its seven heads and ten horns, as it will represent eight kingdoms. It will then be possible to count the number of a man and a beast, which will be studied in a later chapter.

Not all kingdoms in the Bible are called "beasts" although the eight kingdoms that belong to Leviathan are evil and each are referred to as being a beast. These are some of the most exciting pieces of the puzzle that will be added to the foundation. To summarize: the horns and heads are kings and kingdoms. However, what is their significance? Are they joined to something that will give a better understanding of their true meaning? I would like to take you back to the Old Testament where we read a name that few understand. I am now going to lay this piece of the puzzle to the premise concerning Leviathan, a dragon that lives in the sea but not the kind of dragon that one would normally think of. Through study it is revealed that this sea serpent is the same in the Old Testament as it is in the New Testament. We are going to chase after this beast and study its ten horns (ten kings) that at one time figuratively sat upon one of Leviathan's seven heads (Dan. 7:20), ruling that kingdom. Understand, when studying Leviathan, all ten horns are crowned along with its seven heads, which gives authority to this satanic beast. These are some of the most exciting pieces of the puzzle as a foundation begins to form.

- A beast equals a kingdom and includes people, armies, a king or kings and their philosophy of life.

- A horn equals a king and horns equal kings.

- A head equals a mountain and a mountain equals a beast or kingdom of power, pride and evil.

- Leviathan is shown as a metaphorical symbolic sea beast that consists of seven heads and ten horns with a body and tail. When I refer to a head, I am referring to one of the heads of Leviathan, representing a kingdom.

- Leviathan continues from the Old Testament into the New Testament.

- All kingdoms that belong to Leviathan are blasphemous.

- Leviathan's heads and horns are crowned, which gives authority.

- Leviathan's ten horns will be used to destroy a great city.

Let's examine the next several chapters that will lift the mystery of this great powerful sea beast. This study will become repetitious and without doing so Leviathan will not be grasped.

Chapter 5

Leviathan – The Bible's Darkest Metaphor

God gave us the most complicated complex metaphor ever entered into the Bible, that of Leviathan. This metaphor has affected history beyond any other and will eventually have a role in every soul on earth. From Genesis to Revelation, Leviathan has interacted not only with mankind, but also with heavenly angels described in the twelfth chapter of Revelation. God put this power into play, but for what reason? Had he predetermined this powerful red dragon to be used for his purpose?

"And another sign appeared in heaven: behold, a great, fiery red dragon having seven heads and ten horns, and seven diadems on his heads. V4 His tail drew a third of the stars of heaven and threw them to earth" (Rev. 12:3-4).

This great fiery dragon was so powerful that it deceived one third of heavens angels that had an allegiance to God and were considered trusting and pure. They eventually faced a force of immense power and deceit as Leviathan separated the true from the false. Symbolically, its tail was used against the angels. The serpent's heads and horns are crowned with authority and will be used not only against God's chosen ones, but also the entire world.

In the Epistle of Jude, beginning with verse 6, we are informed that God's eternal angels did not keep their rightful place in heaven. They gave themselves over to sexual immorality and chased after strange flesh. These fallen angels will suffer the vengeance of eternal fire. In Genesis 6, men on earth produced daughters. The sons of God found these earthly women beautiful and freely took them as wives. Their offspring are said to be giants and the world became evil because of this great red dragon and the great dragon Satan. Because of the lust of angels, offspring of pure evil walked the earth. The flesh of men and the spirit of angels were not to mix. This is when the flood enters the picture, erasing all evil with the exception of eight righteous souls.

- "May those curse it who curse the day, Those who are ready to arouse Leviathan" (Job 3.8).
- "In that day the Lord with His severe sword, great and strong, Will punish Leviathan the fleeing serpent, Leviathan that twisted serpent; And He will slay the reptile that *is* in the sea" (Isa. 27:1).
- "You broke the heads of Leviathan in pieces, *And* gave him *as* food to the people inhabiting the wilderness" (Ps. 74:14).
- "There the ships sail about; *There* is that Leviathan Which You have made to play there" (Ps. 104:26).

Psalm 74:14 gives us a clue as to the elements of this metaphor. Leviathan has more than one head, as "heads" the plural was used in this verse. Leviathan is also portrayed as a serpent that lives in the sea, (Isa. 27:1, Ps. 104:26 and Rev. 13:1.) My premise: this is the same beast with seven heads and ten horns that supports the harlot, the great city of trade found in Revelation 17 and 18.

Why Other Concepts Have Not Unlocked Revelation

Many past illustrations have portrayed a great sea beast rising up out of the sea having seven heads and ten horns as viewed in Revelation 13:1 and given the name of Leviathan, even though the depiction connects the name to the Old Testament. When it comes to Job 41, the name is rarely connected to Revelation, especially in recent days. Many cannot fathom the thought that this metaphor moves from the Old Testament into the New Testament. God has done a tremendous job to confound even the brightest of minds. He accomplished this by scattering clues throughout the Bible, connections relating to the sea beast. These clues obscured the metaphor that could have been understood many generations ago. As we now see, not until the time of the end would this powerful metaphor become drawn together, assembled to the point of unveiling its mystery. God has a time table to unveil the last book in the Bible.

In the past, there have been bits and pieces gathered to give a degree of understanding, especially Revelation's first four chapters. Even at the end of the fourth chapter there are those that have injected conjecture, setting a foundation without scripture, referring to a taking up, a removal of the saints, although when researching Revelation we find just the opposite view. Throughout the Bible tribulation is accepted, even to the point of death. Many times proving one's faith is expected by God. Are you worthy to receive a crown of eternal life? Many believe he will keep true believers from his wrath. This is where the word "rapture" quickly enters and connects to the removal of the saints. The misconception doesn't mean that the saints won't be faced with the wrath of man and Satan. In fact, it is stated there will be Christians here at the time of the Lord's return and this is fiercely debated by those that embrace the rapture which will be discussed in a later chapter.

More confusion has been added to the mound of writings, proclaiming the great tribulation is historical and ended with the fall of Rome. Others say there are many raptures and the first one has already taken place. The truth of the harlot, Mystery Babylon, the great city Babylon has also been so totally obscured. To the extent that no one can make sense of its symbolism. The seventeenth chapter of Revelation was the only chapter used in trying to reveal the true conception of this great city. With the connection of the eighteenth chapter, only then do the lights begin to glow, finding that the harlot represents a trade city. Revelation's fourteenth chapter gives a chronological order of when this city is to be destroyed.

The book of Revelation is no different than a combination to a safe. Imagine each number representing scripture that not only has to be laid in sequence, as in the seven seals, trumpet and bowl judgments. It also has to be understood without paradox. When entering the world of eschatology, all the facts must be based from scripture for deciphering and verifying for what is being declared. In order to achieve the ultimate goal of seeking biblical truth, one must use scripture and not conjecture.

God Humbles Job

The book of Job is considered to be the oldest book in the Bible. If so, the metaphor Leviathan has been with us from the very beginning as it has everything to do with the fall of the angels and the fall of mankind.

"May those curse it who curse the day, those who are ready to arouse Leviathan" (Job 3.8).

I find it strange that Job used Leviathan as he cursed himself. Did he really understand this metaphor? God then challenged him. Let's begin with Job 41.

"Can you draw out Leviathan with a hook, Or *snare* his tongue with a line *which* you lower? V2 Can you put a reed through his nose, Or pierce his jaw with a hook? V3 Will he make many supplications to you? Will he speak softly to you? V4 Will he make a covenant with you? Will you take him as a servant forever? V5 Will you play with him as *with* a bird, Or will you leash him for your maidens? V6 Will *your* companions make a banquet of him? Will they apportion him among the merchants? V7 Can you fill his skin with harpoons, Or his head with fishing spears? V8 Lay your hand on him; Remember the battle — Never do it again! V9 Indeed, *any* hope of *overcoming* him is false;

Shall *one not* be overwhelmed at the sight of him? V10 No one *is so* fierce that he would dare stir him up. Who then is able to stand against Me? V11 Who has preceded Me, that I should pay *him*? Everything under heaven is Mine. V12 I will not conceal his limbs, His mighty power, or his graceful proportions" (Job 41:1-12).

Just think how God affected Job as question after question flowed into his ears to which he could not answer.

"V13 Who can remove his outer coat? Who can approach *him* with a double bridle? V14 Who can open the doors of his face, *With* his terrible teeth all around? V15 *His* rows of scales are *his* pride, Shut up tightly *as with* a seal; V16 One is so near another That no air can come between them; V17 They are joined one to another; They stick together and cannot be parted. V18 His sneezings flash forth light, And his eyes *are* like the eyelids of the morning. V19 Out of his mouth go burning lights; Sparks of fire shoot out. V20 Smoke goes out of his nostrils, As *from* a boiling pot and burning rushes. V21 His breath kindles coals, And a flame goes out of his mouth. V22 Strength dwells in his neck, And sorrow dances before him (Job 41:13-22).

In part, God is giving us a perception of a fire breathing dragon. The scales on this beast protect it, and also make it prideful.

"V23 The folds of his flesh are joined together; They are firm on him and cannot be moved. V24 His heart is as hard as stone, Even as hard as the lower *millstone*. V25 When he raises himself up, the mighty are afraid; Because of his crashings they are beside themselves. V26 *Though* the sword reaches him, it cannot avail; Nor does spear, dart, or javelin. V27 He regards iron as straw, *And* bronze as rotten wood. V28 The arrow cannot make him flee; Slingstones become like stubble to him. V29 Darts are regarded as straw; He laughs at the threat of javelins. V30 His undersides *are* like sharp potsherds; He spreads pointed *marks* in the mire. V 31 He makes the deep boil like a pot; He makes the sea like a pot of ointment. V32 He leaves a shining wake behind him; *One* would think the deep had white hair. V33 On the earth there is nothing like him, Which is made without fear. V34 He beholds every high *thing*; He is king over all the children of pride" (Job. 41:23-34).

Job acknowledged to God that he did not know what this fire-breathing beast actually signified. He could not give an answer to something he could not understand. The only way this verse can be understood is that "he is king over all the children of pride." As this metaphor unfolds, Leviathan will be portrayed as nations of pride, power and evil.

Are Job 40 and 41 Representing the Same Beast?

Let's view another piece of the puzzle that removes more of the mystery and that is the behemoth of Job 40. Are Chapters 40 and 41 describing two different beasts? I believe the mystery of the behemoth is no different than Leviathan because the language is similar. Both chapters inform us that it is futile for man to raise a sword against either of these powerful beasts. Do we now have two beasts that no man can kill, or two metaphors that shroud one beast?

The New Unger's Bible Dictionary lists the behemoth and Leviathan.

- behemoth – water ox, the hippopotamus or Nile horse.
- Leviathan – is a "mourning, wreathed animal"; a serpent, crocodile, large sea monster and the constellation of the dragon.

Is it the Nile horse, a hippopotamus that lurks in the river bottom portraying the behemoth? The problem is that humans can kill a beast like this. However, it is stated that God is the only one that can bring it down. It has to be figurative! So, what does the behemoth actually represent?

"Look now at the behemoth, which I made *along* with you; He eats grass like an ox. V16 See now, his strength *is* in his hips, And his power *is* in his stomach muscles. V17 He moves his tail like a cedar; The sinews of his thighs are tightly knit. V18 His bones *are like* beams of bronze, His ribs like bars of iron. V19 He *is* the first of the ways of God; Only He who made him can bring near his sword. V20 Surely the mountains yield food for him, And all the beasts of the field play there. V21 He lies under the lotus trees, In a covert of reeds and marsh. V22 The lotus trees cover him *with* their shade; The willows by the brook surround him. V23 Indeed the river may rage, *Yet* he is not disturbed;

He is confident, though the Jordan gushes into his mouth, V24 *Though* he takes it in his eyes, Or one pierces *his* nose with a snare" (Job 40:15–24).

What do we know about the behemoth? We know that this beast is very strong and created by God and was the first of his ways, this is absolutely amazing! For an eternity, nothing has been compared to the likeness of Leviathan. It is the first of its kind. This great beast was made along with Job (mankind) and mountains (kingdoms), and will yield food this serpent. Since the hippopotamus can be killed and does not have a tail that moves like a cedar tree, I would then assume God is referring to Leviathan as being first of its kind. With symbolism, Job writes of a powerful beast that lies under the lotus tree and is covered by it as well as the reeds and marsh. He is not bothered as the Jordan gushes into his mouth. What is the significance of this beast and do we really understand the interpretation of this writing? Let's take scripture from Ezekiel 29:3-7, and compare its symbolic writing to Job, Chapter 41. If we had not been informed that the great river monster represented Pharaoh, King of Egypt, we would run into the same problem as in the Book of Job when comparing the behemoth to Leviathan. Even though Ezekiel's metaphorical language compares to Job 40 and 41, Pharaohs have been killed by men, so it would be impossible for them to represent the behemoth or Leviathan, stating no man can kill these beasts. Only through God is Leviathan brought down.

Job 40:17 describes the behemoth's tail moving like a cedar tree. Does Leviathan's tail sweep back and forth like the dragon's tail described in the twelfth chapter of Revelation, drawing a third of God's angels down to earth? Does this dragon capture souls by sweeping its tail throughout the universe, deceiving those with its awesome power and glittery lies? I believe so!

An important question: before the flood, were the angels the cause of man's sin, or actually was it Leviathan that tested them, separating the true believer from the false? After this, God said he was sorry that he had made man and sent a flood to destroy the evil that persisted in mankind. Was he surprised that his eternal angels fell to evil? 1 John 3:8 explains why Jesus was sent and that is to destroy the works of the devil.

My conclusion: It seems the behemoth is an adjective expressing a noun. Job 40 describes a beast of immense power and the behemoth does represent a powerful beast and the power of man does not disturb it. Only later in the next chapter, Job 41, is the behemoth given the proper name of Leviathan and portrayed as king over all the children of pride. On the other hand, none will understand until the end times and for the first time in history Leviathan is slowly being drawn out into the light, so let's review important pieces of the puzzle.

- The behemoth is an adjective expressing a noun. In Job 41 this serpent receives a proper name of Leviathan.
- Job could not understand the metaphor Leviathan and became humbled.
- Leviathan is king over all the children of pride.
- The behemoth describes a powerful beast. Its tail moves like a cedar tree and this connects to Rev. 12:3-4. Figuratively, its tail collected a third of God's heavenly angels and cast them to earth.
- No man can penetrate its scales or kill Leviathan, only God can.
- Leviathan is portrayed as a sea serpent, a great beast or fire breathing dragon, (Job 40-41, Isa. 27:1, Rev. 13:1).
- Leviathan has seven heads and ten horns (Revelation, chapters 12, 13 and 17).
- Leviathan consists of eight beasts (Rev. 17:11).
- Leviathan's reach extends to heaven (Rev. 12:3-4).
- God's Leviathan is the first of his kind (Job 40:19).

When Leviathan rises up out of the sea all seven heads are exposed, (Rev 13:1). Ten horns are also included and represent a kingdom that was ruled by ten kings, (Dan: 7:20). This kingdom is prophesied to return and will become the eighth. This is the last kingdom that makes up Leviathan, (Rev. 17:11).

"When he raises himself up, the mighty are afraid; Because of his crashings they are beside themselves" (Job 41:25)

"And four great beasts came up from the sea, each different from the other" (Dan. 7:3).

These four kingdoms (beasts) are one half of Leviathan, the last half. They are the lion, bear, leopard and the ten horns. Figuratively, while Leviathan stays submerged all its kingdoms are from the sea and are the makeup of this beast, yet all its kingdoms originate from the earth.

"Those great beasts, which *are* four, are four kings *which* arise out of the earth" (Dan. 7:17).

As we study Leviathan, we see its heads or kingdoms rise from the earth, and when Leviathan goes into the sea, they are said to be from the sea and are said to be hidden. The truth is that Leviathan's heads have been hidden in a figurative sea for over two thousand years has confused scholars. They could never understand how these beasts (kingdoms) are from the earth, yet from the sea. They belong to the sea beast Leviathan.

This metaphorical fire-breathing dragon is exceedingly prideful, powerful and deceitful and has directly caused the fall of a third of heaven's angels and mankind. This led to the mix of earthly women and fallen angels, all because of lust. Their offspring have spread evil throughout the earth. This slithering serpent leaves a shining wake behind him with a wonderment of power along with sinful luring knowledge to dazzle those that have no idea of connecting the evil that flows from it. This is why God brought this metaphorical power into existence. Those that love the excitement of power, pride and evil see a glittery side to all this, they will have their day in the sun and sadly condemn themselves for an eternity.

"In that day the Lord with His severe sword, great and strong, Will punish Leviathan the fleeing serpent, Leviathan that twisted serpent; And He will slay the reptile that *is* in the sea" (Isa. 27:1).

Before the Lord's return, this sea beast will be involved in the last great war named Armageddon. At this time Leviathan will not escape God's hand.

Leviathan is written like that of a caterpillar turning into a beautiful butterfly, but there is one huge difference. This beast will eventually destroy the world. The metamorphosis of Leviathan connects to Daniel, as he was told that he would not understand it. Only at the end of times would it be understood. We now know that the end is about to begin. In the early stage of Leviathan, this creature was known as a fire breathing dragon. Isaiah addressed it as a serpent or reptile that lives in the sea. Psalm 74:14 changes the structure of this serpent and informs us that this living thing has more than one head. Now this beast moves from the Old Testament into the New Testament. With the introduction of Revelation 12:3 and 13:1, there is an understanding that this serpent has seven heads and also its ten horns are introduced. Yet, Leviathan is not fully assembled. This metaphorical sea beast now transforms into eight literal kingdoms that are not godly. Job described this beast as a powerful fire breathing dragon and refers more to the cover of this book. With study, Leviathan eventually turns into a collection of kings and kingdoms. Pride power and evil are its attributes.

Chapter 6

Two Dreams – Unveiling Leviathan

Let's take a look at how tradition has played a role in the hindrance to fully comprehending this powerful sea beast. The Jewish Tanach, along with the Bible, gives a perfect example of commentaries to which I believe are in great error. Without being connected to Revelation it would be impossible to understand Job's Leviathan. Between Daniel and Revelation there is enough critical information collected which eventually gives up the mystery of these two elusive metaphors. The first is Leviathan and the second is a harlot named "Mystery Babylon" to which this figurative sea serpent supports, as evil supports evil. Before separating their components, two very important dreams have to be scrutinized. Without comprehending these exceptional dreams, the chase for Leviathan would be futile. Let's make an observation of Daniel interpreting King Nebuchadnezzar's dream of a statue.

I would like to express that many chapters are written in numerical value (like the number 8, instead of being spelled out as "eight"). I believe it is much easier to retain scripture.

"You, O king, were watching; and behold, a great image! This great image, whose splendor *was* excellent, stood before you; and its form *was* awesome" (Dan. 2:31).

Daniel's comment was extremely interesting. He praised the image to which the king was included and revealed the awesome dream that represented a statue made in four sections, representing four kingdoms. Yet, Daniel withdrew his awe-inspiring comments when he had a dream or vision of four kingdoms. The last kingdom of his vision, the ten horns, shook him with fear. Although Daniel commented on the king's inspiring dream, unknowing to him it would come to be that all four kingdoms represented by the statue, would eventually enslave his people, the ones of Jewish blood. Daniel's vision was to be far beyond his lifetime and Nebuchadnezzar's dream of his awesome statue concluded with the fall of Rome. The importance of the king's dream along with Daniel's mysterious dream is that the mystery would be not be unveiled until the end times and then would be joined to the apostle John's, the book of Revelation.

Many Bible commentaries state that Daniel's vision in Daniel, Chapter 7, is just a recap of King Nebuchadnezzar's dream in Chapter 2. In other words, the statue that is divided into four sections is representing the same kingdoms in both chapters. Why would this be significant? Is the interpretation accurate and are there only four kingdoms or actually eight? Does this relate to Revelation's sea beast with seven heads and ten horns, illuminating a total count of eight kingdoms? Let's compare both dreams and see if the biblical commentaries have been in error.

The King's Dream – Daniel, Chapter 2

- First section. The head made of fine gold – representing King Nebuchadnezzar and Babylon.

- Second section. Chest and arms made of silver – representing Persia.

- Third section. Belly and thighs made of bronze – representing Greece and Alexander the Great.

- Fourth section. Legs of iron and feet mixed with iron and clay, representing Rome, (Daniel 2:32-33).

Daniel's Vision – Daniel, Chapter 7

- First beast. Kingdom represented by a lion, (Dan. 7:4).
- Second beast. Kingdom represented by a bear, Dan. (7:5).
- Third beast. Kingdom represented by a leopard, (Dan. 7:6).
- Fourth beast. Kingdom represented by ten horns that will become active and rule the entire world. This beast is extremely different from the other kingdoms. A king will rule this kingdom and will be different from the other kings, (Daniel 7:7, 19–25).

Are both dreams representing a same fourth kingdom? Is Daniel's dream the same as Nebuchadnezzar's? Many commentaries say they are; scripture says the opposite.

Throughout centuries the quest for Leviathan stayed elusive. No one has been able to identify or verify what this metaphor represents. More than likely, it had been passed over millions of times without comprehending what was read. The beast's seven heads and ten horns mentioned in Revelation actually lie between the pages of Daniel's book. By combining both dreams in Daniel, Chapters 2 and 7, seven kingdoms (beasts) and ten kings (ten horns) emerge. Daniel 7 informs us that the ten horns represent a beast or kingdom, along with a king that is different from all other kings. We now have a total count of eight kingdoms. This is the exact number of beasts or kingdoms that are expressed in Revelation 17:11. Again, do both dreams represent the same kingdoms? Let's begin to cross-reference the dreams.

Nebuchadnezzar's Dream –Statue Representing Four Kingdoms

Babylon is represented by the statue's head made of fine gold; the first of four kingdoms. When being cross-referenced with the first kingdom of Daniel's vision we see a lion with eagle's wings. The great wings would denote power and swiftness. I immediately found the comparison odd. Why weren't the other three kingdoms of Nebuchadnezzar's statue represented by eagle wings, as they moved faster and became more powerful? Persia defeated Babylon, Greece defeated Persia and so on. Each kingdom surpassed the other as they descended down to the legs and feet, ending with Rome.

Persia represents the second kingdom of Nebuchadnezzar's statue, with its chest and arms made of silver. When cross-referenced to the second kingdom in Daniel's vision we see a bear raised up on its side with three ribs in its mouth, between its teeth, and was told to devour much flesh. It seems the bear destroys part of its own infrastructure, holding three of its ribs in its mouth and being raised up only on one side. I found nothing that would support Ancient Persia's history symbolizing a bear with three ribs in its mouth. In Chapter 8 of Daniel, two kings (Cyrus and Darius) are portrayed as a ram with two horns. This would represent Media and Persia.

Greece, represented by Alexander the Great, the third kingdom of Nebuchadnezzar's statue, represented by its belly and thighs are made of bronze. Now another problem rises. When cross-referenced with Daniel's vision, Alexander is supposedly compared to a leopard. Chapter 8 of Daniel informs us that Alexander is actually represented as a male goat with a large horn, not a leopard and will kill the ram with two horns.

Rome, the last kingdom of Nebuchadnezzar's dream includes legs, feet and toes. When cross-referenced with the last kingdom in Daniel's vision it is described as ten horns, belonging on the head and not the feet as in the king's fourth kingdom. Even if the horns were on Nebuchadnezzar's head of fine gold, historically I found nothing referring to a total count of ten kings that would connect to Babylon. God also stated that this kingdom would never rise again. The legs are of iron but the foundation is mixed with a weakness using clay. The feet and toes are also mixed with iron and clay. As in the potter's wheel, clay can be reshaped unlike iron and can become a threat to mighty Rome. Let's see if clarity can be given to the feet and toes.

"And as the toes of the feet *were* partly of iron and partly of clay, so the kingdom shall be partly strong and partly fragile. V43 As you saw iron mixed ceramic clay, they will mingle with the seed of men; but they will not adhere to one another, just as iron does not mix with clay. V44 And in the days of these kings the God of heaven will set up a kingdom which shall never be destroyed; and the kingdom shall not be left to other people; it shall break in pieces and consume all these kingdoms, and it shall stand forever. V45 Inasmuch as you saw that the stone was cut out of the mountain without hands, and that it broke in pieces the iron, the bronze, the clay, the silver, and the gold – the great God has made known to the king what will come to pass after this. The dream is certain, and the interpretation is sure" (Dan. 2:42-45).

A kingdom will be established that will never be destroyed. The one that will be ahead of this kingdom is a cornerstone cut from a mountain and without hands. God establishes his kingdom through the blood of Jesus and this took place at the time of these kings, representing the Roman Empire. With the fall of all four kingdoms, Nebuchadnezzar's dream comes to a close and Daniels book is to be sealed. God's plan succeeded in keeping a remnant from the time of Babylon's conquest over Judah, eventually placing Jesus at the head of his kingdom. In this same time frame, scripture referring to the time of Rome is simply stating that the toes, which are part of the feet, described in Dan. 2:41, are mixed with potter's clay and iron and will not adhere to one another. I do not believe the toes are referring to ten kingdoms that founded the Roman Empire and the number "ten" is not entered. The toes, feet and legs are in reference to the time of Rome being mixed with believers and those that will never accept the Son of God.

"Then the iron, then clay, the bronze, the silver, and the gold were crushed together, and became like chaff from the summer threshing floors; the wind carried them away so that no trace of them was found. And the stone that struck the image became a great mountain and filled the whole earth" (Dan. 2:35).

There are negatives of both dreams representing the same kingdoms. Beginning with Daniel 7:7, he considered the ten horns and understood they were different from the lion, bear and leopard. Daniel 7:12 gives more indication to support the premise. *This is important to understand!* The last kingdom, the ten horns are destroyed first and the remaining three kingdoms (lion, bear and leopard) lives are spared but have no dominion. This did not take place in the king's dream. Nebuchadnezzar's statue represented nations that were destroyed in succession. Another very important fact: the lion, bear, leopard and ten horns are figurative, representing real kingdoms. Yet, horns do not belong to the first three beasts of Daniels dream. The last beast of Daniel 7 is different from the others, and comes from the lands of the leopard. These horns have to be so intertwined with the character of Satan that they are of one spirit, of one mind.

Revelation 17 informs us that these ten horns are kings without a kingdom, but at an appointed time they will join or become active with the beast or kingdom from which they originated. In other words, an old kingdom revives and becomes a new kingdom that will eventually devour the earth. The ten horns of Daniel 7:20 represent ten kings that at one time ruled a kingdom. Over two thousand years pass and horns will once again interact with the beast, only to destroy the harlot in Revelation, Chapters 17 and 18, and then overcome the world. Figuratively, the entire beast will be engaged with its horns and then conquer the world.

Once again let's review each dream and compare them side by side. This is of utmost importance to anyone seriously trying to understand the clues that help unlock Revelation. Keep in mind that many teachers of eschatology express that these two dreams are identical, representing the same kingdoms. I think you will agree that there is a problem with this view.

Is there a significant reason why both dreams have a fourth kingdom that dominate world powers? Are they identical kingdoms of the same time period? Again, God lets confusion creep in as the vast majority believed Rome was the kingdom that was prophesied to return and that Daniel's vision supported it.

"And the fourth kingdom shall be as strong as iron, inasmuch as iron breaks in pieces and shatters everything; and like iron that crushes, *that kingdom* will break in pieces and crush all the others. V41 Whereas you saw the feet and the toes, partly of potter's clay, and partly of iron, the kingdom shall be divided; yet the strength of the iron shall be in it, just as you saw the iron mixed with the ceramic clay. V42 And *as* the toes and the feet *were* partly of iron and partly of clay, *so* the kingdom shall be partly strong and partly fragile. V43 As you saw iron mixed with ceramic clay, they will mingle with the seed of men; but they will not adhere to one another, just as iron does not mix with clay" (Daniel 2:40–43).

These last verses explain that there is division in the Roman Empire. It's foundation is mixed. Let's go to Daniel's vision and try to understand the last of his four kingdoms, the ten horns.

"Then I wished to know the truth about the fourth beast, which was different from all the others, exceedingly dreadful, *with* its teeth of iron and its nails of bronze, *which* devoured, broke in pieces, and trampled the residue with its feet; V20 and the ten horns that *were* on its head, and the other *horn* which came up, before which three fell, namely, that horn which had eyes and a mouth which spoke pompous words, whose appearance *was* greater than his fellows" (Dan. 7:19–20).

There are similarities and differences between the two kingdoms. All Nebuchadnezzar's kingdoms are represented by metals from the earth and as we descend the statue the metals increase in strength. Each kingdom becomes stronger. The statues fourth kingdom included clay and this would not adhere to iron. Daniel's four kingdoms are portrayed by beasts, animals. The ten horns are different and seen by themselves. Yet with the blessing of God they will become active and join the head and body of the beast.

Nebuchadnezzar was directly affected by his dream, unlike Daniel's dream, which was beyond his lifetime. After his death many centuries would pass and not until the time of the end would there be a comprehension of what he wrote (Dan. 12:4, 7-9).

Nebuchadnezzar's Fourth Kingdom

- God establishes his kingdom through his son Jesus at the time of Rome.
- Strong as iron.
- Legs of iron, feet and toes of iron and clay.

- Crushes kingdoms.
- Kingdom divided—partly strong and partly fragile as it is partly iron and clay.

Daniel's Fourth Kingdom

- Exceedingly dreadful.
- Teeth of iron and nails of bronze. There is no mention of gold or iron mixed with clay or weakness in Daniel's vision.
- Devours the whole earth, tramples it and breaks it into pieces.
- Ten horns *were* on a head, Dan. 7:20, as opposed to Nebuchadnezzar's fourth kingdom, mentioning only the legs, feet and toes Dan.2:42.
- Another horn (king) comes up and kills three of the ten horns (kings) and becomes greater than the other horns and speaks pompous words against the highest one. The saints are given into his hand for three and a half years. Which is forty-two months.
- Daniel's fourth kingdom, the ten horns, is not divided and all think alike (Rev. 17:12-13).
- Daniel 7:23, expresses that Daniel's fourth kingdom is very different from the other three.
- Daniel's fourth kingdom (ten horns) is destroyed first while the other three lives (lion, bear and leopard) are spared for a short time and will be without dominion.

The beast's ten horns are portrayed by themselves. It seems as though they are independent of the beast to which they belong, yet they will engage with the entire body as described in Revelation 17:12-13. King Nebuchadnezzar statue's head is made of fine gold. Daniel's vision has ten horns and no toes are mentioned. Nebuchadnezzar's statue did not portray ten horns, which would have represented ten horns (kings) upon the head of gold. Yet, Daniel's vision describes teeth made of iron, unlike Nebuchadnezzar's head, which was of fine gold. Daniel sees nails of bronze and Nebuchadnezzar's breast and arms were made of silver. In Daniel's fourth and last kingdom there is no mention of clay mixed with iron and speaks of no weakness. In Nebuchadnezzar's last kingdom some Romans converted to Christianity. The lowest section of the statue was partly strong and partly fragile, unlike Daniel's fourth, the ten horns are seen with no division (Rev. 17:12–13). Nebuchadnezzar's fourth kingdom represents Ancient Rome and the saints are mixed with this kingdom for centuries. This is contrary to the ten horns, as their kingdom will not mix with the saints and are of one mind and have an agenda. This is to destroy the great city of New York, along with believers of the true God! These two dreams are describing different kingdoms in completely different time periods. Each kingdom in Nebuchadnezzar's dream fell in succession as prophesied, one battled against the other until Rome was the last of the kingdoms to fall. Only one of these kingdoms is prophesied to return. A kingdom that will not assimilate to other religions. This kingdom revives and comes from King Nebuchadnezzar's dream of a statue.

"Then the iron, the clay, the bronze, the silver and the gold were crushed together, and became like chaff from the summer threshing floors; the wind carried them away so that no trace of them was found. And the stone that struck the image became a great mountain and filled the whole earth" (Dan. 2:35).

All four ancient kingdoms are destroyed with one exception. A kingdom will rise from where the first ten horns originated and then terrorize the world. They will rule a revived kingdom. Unlike the king's dream, the ten horns take over the entire earth and this is an end time prophecy.

Leviathan is a collection of kings and kingdoms, all with pride, power and evil. No man can defeat it except the one who has created it, the almighty God himself. By combining both dreams we now see a collection of eight kingdoms: Babylon, Persia, Greece, Rome, lion, bear, leopard and ten horns. One of the first four kingdoms was ruled by ten kings (Dan. 7:20). Persia, the second head of Leviathan is the only ancient kingdom that connects to the ten horns, which is now modern day Iran. This nation constantly chants "Death to America." They also eye America's great city of New York and mark it for total destruction. This city is the top of their agenda. Daniel and John's warning of ten kings destroying this great city is yet to come.

Rome, grand and powerful, was no different than the other three preceding kingdoms, unlike Daniel's diverse fourth kingdom which is prophesied to flourish once again. Revelation, Chapter 17, gives clues and information on the return of the ten horns, the kingdom (beast) that was and will be.

As the Second World War drew to an end, Leviathan was once again called upon to become aroused, (Job 3:8) to destroy the Jews before they once again gathered to become one people in one land. Many ancient foes surrounded them as skirmishes began to rise, trying to drive out any that were helping to create a new Jewish State. With God's grace, in 1948 Arab land once again became Jewish land.

Leviathan has tainted the heavens with evil. This metaphorical beast has also been called upon to destroy God's truth, along with his prophesied remnant, the 144,000 Jews. There are 12,000 from each of the twelve tribes. These are God's elect that are pure and follow the lamb Jesus, and is referenced in Revelation's fourteenth chapter.

Satan and Leviathan have a major objective and that is to eliminate the Jew and bring down the Christian. To review, my premise begins with the Book of Daniel (Chapter 2) and Nebuchadnezzar's dream of a statue representing four kingdoms; Babylon, Persia, Greece and Rome. Daniel's vision gives light to four more kingdoms represented by a lion, bear, leopard and ten horns. These two dreams are very different and do not represent the same kingdoms, with the exception of one that has a connection to its past, Persia. The old kingdom is dust, yet its threads connect to a new kingdom that is now beginning to rise.

Does China Belong To Leviathan?

I believe China could be one of the three leopard heads that will give the crowned leopard its dominance as described in Dan. 7:6. Revelation 12:3 informs us that all Leviathan's seven heads are crowned and that would leave three leopard heads giving power and dominance to the crowned leopard. Could this nation have the ability to raise an army of two hundred million as referenced in Revelation 9:16? This connects to the sixth trumpet and bowl judgment. Short of a nuclear war or an act of God, an army this size would be impossible to stop. This nation has never connected to Nebuchadnezzar's dream and had no part of the old kingdoms. Although, I believe they will play a role with their newly acquired technology, much of it developed by the United States. China has nothing to do with the ten horns, but as the horns consume the lion, bear and leopard, as described in Daniel 7, the entire world will succumb to this beast and that would include China. Historically, they have killed Christians but have never dominated the twelve tribes of Israel. It is not one of the beasts in Nebuchadnezzar's dream. This nation more than likely will help the ten horns fulfill their domination and participate in the great tribulation. Revelation's thirteenth chapter will enlighten us to who is involved in dominating the world in the very last days.

Chapter 7

Egypt is not Part of Leviathan

Why is it impossible for Assyria or Egypt to represent one of the heads of Leviathan? Egypt invited God's chosen into their country and as it turned out they became heavily yoked into bondage and forced to learn and accept different gods. The Jews eventually lost their true path as they bowed to false teachings. The price they paid for this was dreadful. Although God promised Abraham and his descendants that they would beget great nations, there was a stipulation attached to this. God clearly expressed that they had to keep his covenant. Years later, Moses leads them from captivity to the promise land. King Solomon was chosen by God to build his temple, which should have led the Jewish tribes in a true spirit. This came to full term with creating the nation of Israel. This was the fulfillment of God's promise to Abraham. When King David's grandson Rehoboam became king, it caused a split. This took place around 930 B.C.. Ten of the twelve tribes became the Northern Kingdom named Israel. The last two tribes became the Southern Kingdom, known as Judah. They began to battle as Judah tried to turn them from the evil ways they acquired, but could not. The ten tribes became an abomination as they turned to other gods and later so did the Kingdom of Judah (Jeremiah 3:8). Because of Israel's backsliding, God gave them a certificate of divorce, breaking a covenant that the Northern Kingdom did not hold worthy. Yet, Judah did not fear retribution, so they continued to play a despised and cursed harlot. God then proclaimed Judah as being the worse of the two, although he did offer a reprieve. Only if they would turn back to righteousness then he would again bless them. However, the offer was rejected. He then brings the Assyrians to the doorstep of the Northern ten tribes. Their governance was no different than the previous Egyptian domination. Although some believe they were worse as they went on to defeat the Northern Kingdom. The ten tribes never recovered to their former glory. The vine of Israel was severed and dispersed throughout the lands, only later to become known as the "Lost Ten Tribes of Israel." Never again did they centralize as did the two tribes that made up Judah. Only under Babylonian rule did the tribes of Judah and Benjamin, the Southern Kingdom, repent of their falling away. For the first time since they became a strong nation and the building of Solomon's great temple, God chastised them by using Babylon's great power. This eventually turned Judah back to God unlike the Northern Kingdom which did not repent and was divorced from the promises that God made to them. Not until the very end of time will he purify and restore all the tribes. Under captivity of the Babylonians, Judah once again set high stakes with setting the foundations of the Torah, teaching their writings with inspiration and truth.

The twelve tribes did not consolidate as a nation until the fulfillment of God's promise as they entered the land of Canaan. Shortly after the formation of Israel, corruption crept in as the chosen ones began to chase their own evil desires and did not turn from their sin. God made a covenant with Abraham and this was broken by all of the twelve tribes. So why begin with Babylon as being the first head of Leviathan?

Assyria conquered the northern ten tribes, but had nothing to do with the two southern tribes, Judah and Benjamin. Babylon was the first kingdom to reign over Judah and God had not removed his hand as he promised to the Jewish forefathers. Under captivity, Judah slowly turned back to truth. With the birth of Jesus, he connects back to King David through the lineage of the kings of Judah.

"May those curse it who curse the day, Those who are ready to arouse Leviathan," (Job 3:8).

I believe Satan could not stand the thought of God setting aside a special people and turning them into a nation that would relish words of truth. As the backsliding began, Leviathan was called upon by using those of evil to yoke the Israelites and possibly destroy the seed of God's chosen. This would entirely delight Satan because it would prove that his word is more powerful than that of his creator. God allowed this to happen and to let Leviathan proceed. Unknown to Satan, Judah would be chastised and truth would once again fill the void. Correction would persist through the power of Babylon. I find it interesting that Daniel lived under King Nebuchadnezzar's rule, experiencing the first head of Leviathan.

Isaiah 66:3-4 reveals why the Jewish nation had gone through so much torment, including the holocaust. They will continue to be underfoot of many nations until the fulfillment of the four hundred and ninety years curse that has been placed on them ends. God pleaded with them to return to his righteous ways, but they chose their own paths, their own ways, and chased their own delights. Now he will chose their delusions, bringing fear upon them. From the time of Daniel to the end of the power of Rome the first four heads of Leviathan were called upon to separate the wicked that have misled the Jewish nation and to chastise the Southern Kingdom. This was to bring them back to a righteous path. After the fall of Rome, the Jewish tribes continued to disperse to the four corners of the world as was prophesied.

The next four kingdoms of Daniel's vision in Chapter 7 will be called upon to once again chastise the Jews, but this time the entire world will come under the power of Leviathan. This planet will virtually be consumed by evil, trampled upon, separating the true from false believers. It will eventually end the Gentile rule.

Remarkably, every time a head (kingdom) of Leviathan was used against the Jews, it would eventually lose its dominance. Starting with the second head Persia, it defeats the first head, Babylon. Then the third head, Alexander the Great of Greece defeats the second head, Persia. Rome, the fourth head, defeats the third head, Greece. Hundreds of years later Rome decays from within and is eventually invaded. Even though the second head seemed to be destroyed, it never died and is still breathing and coming back to power. All these heads are designed by God, used by God, and will be terminated by God. Leviathan is God's creation.

Chapter 8

Three Proclaiming Angels

I cannot think of any prophecy that gives a more complete overview and in chronological order than the fourteenth chapter of Revelation with three angels proclaiming to the world, events to which I believe will unfold in my lifetime or shortly after.

"Then I saw another angel flying in the midst of heaven, having the everlasting gospel to preach to those who dwell on the earth — to every nation, tribe, tongue and people -- V7 saying with a loud voice, "Fear God and give glory to Him, for the hour of His judgment has come; and worship Him who made heaven and earth, the sea and springs of water" (Rev. 14:6-7).

The first angel proclaims to the world that every tongue, tribe, nation, all peoples, all dialects will receive the gospel of our Lord, then judgment comes upon mankind as the end begins. This verse connects to Matthew 24:14.

"And another angel followed, saying, "Babylon is fallen, is fallen, that great city, because she has made all nations drink of the wine of the wrath of her fornication" (Rev. 14:8).

The second angel proclaims that Mystery Babylon, the great city is destroyed. With the connection to Revelation's Chapter 18, it becomes apparent that this city represents trade. With its destruction comes the collapse of world trade (Rev. 18:11). This could be contributed to the fact that no one would dare to work in a city after it was destroyed. What happens to this great city could repeat itself to any city that is vital to world trade.

"Then a third angel followed them, saying with a loud voice, "If anyone worships the beast and his image, and receives *his* mark on his forehead or on his hand, V10 he himself shall also drink of the wine of the wrath of God, which is poured out full strength into the cup of His indignation. He shall be tormented with fire and brimstone in the presence of the holy angels and in the presence of the Lamb. V11 And the smoke of their torment ascends forever and ever; and they have no rest day or night, who worshiped the beast and his image, and whoever receives the mark of his name" (Rev. 14:9–11).

Then a voice from heaven declares "Blessed *are* the dead who die in the Lord from now on" (Rev.14:13).

Blessed are those who die in the name of the Lord from there on and do not take the mark of the beast. Do not confuse the "beginning of the end" with the "Day of the Lord." The chronological timing is different. With the proclaiming of the first angel, the realization comes to how close we are to the beginning of these last prophesied events. Most of us do not like giving dates that attempt to pinpoint future prophetic events, and I'm one of them. There is an exception relating to this first proclaiming angel. Before publishing my first book in 2010, Wycliffe, a major Bible translating organization, moved their target date from 2038 to 2025, shortening the process of delivering the gospel to all tongues. Today, more organizations now admit that the gospel could possibly be given to all dialects within a decade or possibly fifteen years after publishing this book. Jesus is nearing the door and all people on earth are close to hearing the proclamation of our Lord's message. Technology has been the key for the increase in delivery.

We are in the last segment of the Gentile rule and many liberal minds believe that it is man and nature that creates every great thing. People speak of "Mother Nature" as though she were the architect of this earth. Man is trying his hardest to replace the truth of God with fables or mythological beings. Doing so, many try to destroy the credibility of Revelation.

"For the time will come when they will not endure sound doctrine, but according to their own desires, *because* they have itching ears, they will heap up for themselves teachers; V4 and they will turn *their* ears away from the truth, and be turned aside to fables" (2 Tim. 4:3–4).

Eventually, biblical scripture will be turned from truth by those that have evil desires and deceitful agendas. They will assure you that when you die there will be absolutely no accountability, especially to a god. Yet, God's true believers will continue to pass on his everlasting words to all that have the eye to see what he has created and an ear to hear and understand the words of truth, so we can understand the Father and the Son, and discern all things spiritual. The faithful believer will inherit the kingdom of God, the ones that have kept his commandments and believe in Jesus.

Thousands have spread the gospel throughout the world, including Billy Graham, and this is what Revelation 14:6-7 portrays. After the gospel has been given to the entire world, to all peoples and tongues, then judgment comes and it begins with the house of the Lord.

"And another angel followed, saying, "Babylon is fallen, is fallen, that great city, because she has made all nations drink of the wine of the wrath of her fornication" (Rev. 14:8). In Greek this word "city" translates as a city or town.

This is extremely important! According to these three proclaiming angels, Mystery Babylon, the great city is destroyed <u>after</u> the gospel is given to the entire earth. To date, this prophecy has not been fulfilled. This verse describes a city and not a kingdom being destroyed. The apocalypse begins with the cities destruction.

The third proclaiming angel lets us connect more of the dots to reveal its message (Rev. 14:9–11). This is a warning to the entire world, to anyone that believes they can outsmart this false religious system and take its mark for a short time and then give it back. Don't risk your soul for this, because whoever does will lose! Whoever takes the mark, his name, his number or image (likeness), whoever worships the beast (kingdom or its system) shall be tormented forever and ever with fire and brimstone and will not rest day or night.

Flavius Josephus, born in Jerusalem just after the resurrection of Christ, became known to many Jews as their greatest general, historian and was also thought to be a priest. He was so respected that the Romans eventually made him an honorary citizen. It is believed that he was in charge of the temple, having a collection of sacred books that became lost after the temple's destruction in 70 AD. In Antiquities, he wrote of when one dies; if an angel takes you by the left hand and leads you down a corridor, you have been judged to eternal damnation. Once there, a fiery worm enters you and there will be no rest day or night (Rev. 14:10–11).

"We are bound to thank God always for you, brethren, as it is fitting, because your faith grows exceedingly, and the love of every one of you all abounds toward each other, V4 so that we ourselves boast of you among the churches of God for your patience and faith in all your persecutions and tribulations that you endure, V5 *which is* manifest evidence of the righteous judgment of God, that you may be counted worthy of the kingdom of God, for which you also suffer; V6 since *it is a* righteous thing with God to repay with tribulation those who trouble you, V7 and to *give* you who are troubled rest with us when the Lord Jesus is revealed from heaven with His mighty angels" (2 Thess. 1:3–7).

"Let no one deceive you by any means; *for that Day will not come* unless the falling away comes first, and the man of sin is revealed, the son of perdition, V4 who opposes and exalts himself above all that is called God or that is worshipped, so that he sits as God in the temple of God, showing himself that he is God" (2 Thess. 2:3–4).

Today, we hear too much preaching that Jesus could appear right at this moment. This is impossible, if these last verses are to be revered. Could Christ return tomorrow, next week, or next year? Not until this prophecy unfolds!

Paul writes to the Thessalonians telling them that there is evidence for them to be counted worthy through enduring their tribulations. He then moves to the future, to the last days. There will be a great apostasy, as the man of perdition is revealed in his attempt to gain God's throne and exalts himself beyond any other. Along with this comes destruction and the killing of the saints (2 Thess. 2:3-4, Rev. 6: 9-11, 13:11-18, 14:9-13, 20:4-6). Those that die in the name of the Lord will then rest from their labors. After the great tribulation and before the thousand year reign of Christ, the great slaughter of saints ends as God prepares his revenge. At the end of his wrath, three demons will gather all nations to come against Israel to fight God's chosen. There will be one last attempt to destroy the elect and this will be directed by the ugliest spirit on earth, Satan himself. He will kill the saints and support a false prophet along with a false religious system that has taken over the world and if God does not stop this, even his elect would be lost. Christ and his legions of angels will then come and destroy the wicked and punish all nations that come against Israel. He will destroy every nation that divides her land.

"*You who are troubled* will be given rest." This mainly comes through death. In the meantime, there will be saints living at the time of the Lord's return, as they are not removed. These are the ones that have endured the great tribulation. The third proclaiming angel warns us to be prepared and not to join the dark side. In the time of great stress, the ones who die in the name of the Lord are called "blessed." All believers have to endure to the end of their life or until Christ returns.

- First proclaiming angel (Rev. 14:6-7): the gospel of the Lord is given to all dialects then judgment begins with the house of God (1 Peter 4:17). Fear him, yet give him glory.

- Second proclaiming angel: Mystery Babylon, the great trade city is destroyed and with it the collapse of world trade. God tries to call his saints out of the city before it is destroyed (Rev. 18:4).

- Third proclaiming angel: separating the wheat from the tare, the true from the false. This begins with a warning to professing believers. If any join with this beast (kingdom) and take its mark on the forehead or right hand they will be tormented forever (Rev. 14:10–11). From there on the ones who die in the lord, professing his name, are called "blessed."

At this time, any that face the great tribulation will have the chance, the privilege, to spend a thousand year reign with Jesus by not denying his divinity. This is when the true believer will submit to God's will and lay down his life for an eternal crown, one's inheritance is an everlasting life (Rev. 20:4-6).

The third proclaiming angel warns us to be prepared — don't join the dark side. Believers have to endure to the end. If they do not endure, torment will be their partner for eternity, forever and ever. There will be no rest, only torment forever and ever and ever.

Chapter 9

Burning of the Harlot – The Great City of Trade

To begin, I would like to profess my love for my country. There is no other place in this world that I have been more proud of than the United States of America! We have had the privilege to worship the true God, mainly without persecution. Regrettably, we have now begun to take a new course. Over the last few decades there has been a change in our mighty nation; a direction of dominating the world through trade. Along with this, the eyes of the world have begun to question our goals. Has power and deceit replaced her glory? Is there a diabolical agenda to control the world by just a select few through the seduction of trade? For many years I consumed a tremendous amount of biblical information, especially in the realm of eschatology. After studying Mystery Babylon, the great city, the great harlot of Revelation, I gained insight to what this city symbolized and the chilling parallel between two cities. One is ancient and the other sits in the United States. God obscured the truth of this great city until the very end. It should also be noted that the greatest part of Ancient Babylon's power came through trade and was strategically placed alongside the Euphrates River.

"O you who dwell by many waters, Abundant in treasures, Your end has come, The measure of your covetousness" (Jer. 51:13).

Trade increases wealth. Babylon was a splendid city to which all nations, peoples and languages came. Some state that Revelation's "Mystery Babylon," the harlot in Revelation, represents Ancient Babylon. A great city that sat in a great kingdom and was destroyed over two thousand years ago. God proclaimed this city would never rise again. Today there is another great city that parallels Ancient Babylon, a world trade city that now resides on the other side of the world.

Throughout the ages this great city described in Revelation would not compare to any other until January 1, 1995, with the birth of the World Trade Organization. None could conceive the idea of a city that would control world trade, even being that of New York. Until that year, comprehending scripture relating to the harlot could not be achieved until key events paralleled prophecy, only then conjecture would be replaced by a foundation of scripture.

The words of Revelation, especially in Chapters 17 and 18, give clarity to this metaphor when comparing New York City to this harlot.

A whore that nations and kings climb in bed with and fornicate. It is the entire economic system that drives the gears of this great trade city and this also includes Washington D.C. The prophecy of Revelation's great city parallels modern events. Scripture proves this whore cannot represent an ancient city, but rather a city that exists today. Without combining both chapters it is impossible to comprehend this powerful whore that symbolizes a great city that seduces the world through her trade. With the opening of the seventeenth chapter, an angel holding seven bowls came to John and addressed the great harlot, the city that sits on many waters, a city that commits fornication with the inhabitants of earth.

It is claimed by some that this whore represents either Ancient Rome, which has already been destroyed, or a futuristic Rome, returning once again to rule the world. Many believe she is the Roman Catholic Church with the Vatican leading the charge of a New Roman Empire, deceiving the world and later cast into hell. Even the name "Mystery Babylon" connecting to modern Rome should be scrutinized. Some base their premise that the Vatican is the great city. Others claim it is a spiritual city, referring to Revelation's eighteenth chapter. Yet, God proclaims it is an abomination and he calls his saints out of this great city before it is destroyed. The Vatican would be emptied before it was demolished and if destroyed, I don't believe it would collapse world trade. Especially since the World Trade Organization sits in New York City. I would agree that the Vatican, as others, are infused or integrated into this powerful trade system. Revelation 17:18 declares this whore will reign over the kings of the earth and all nations share in her riches. This would not come through the Catholic Church and I cannot fathom Islam being reigned by the Pope. In 2001 terrorists did not go after a religious sector, rather an economic sector. With their ingenious scheming, two impressive trade buildings have been erased. They now have their interest in vaporizing the entire city of New York along with Washington D.C.!

Prophecy leading up to the beginning of the end has not been fulfilled. Several events must unfold before complete chaos comes upon the earth. This begins with the gospel of the Lord given to all peoples, nations, tongues and tribes. Then comes the destruction of the harlot, the great city of trade, triggering the apocalypse. We are within a blink of an eye before all dialects receive the gospel and then judgment will begin.

Let's see if we can separate conjecture from fact.

Why the Harlot cannot Represent Ancient Rome.

- Unlike Rome, three angels proclaim in chronological order that the harlot, Mystery Babylon will not be destroyed until the gospel has been given to all dialects. This has not yet been fulfilled.

- Unlike Rome, she does not see her destruction coming and is destroyed in one day (Rev. 18:7-8).

- Unlike Rome, the harlot reigns over all kings and kingdoms (Rev. 14:8 and 17:18).

- Unlike Rome, the kings of the earth will weep when they see the smoke of her destruction, for there is no more merchandise to be bought with the collapse of world economics. (Rev. 18:9-19).

- Unlike Rome, after her destruction the ones that traded with her will stand at a distance, not daring to come near her (Rev.18:17). This did not happen with the destruction of Ancient Rome. The harlot of Revelation 17 & 18 will die a horrible death by fire, probably caused by a nuclear explosion.

- Unlike Rome, God calls his saints and only his saints out of this city before its total destruction. If they do not leave they will share in the rest of her plagues. Might this be radioactivity? (Rev. 18:4).

- Unlike Rome, this city deceives the world with the help of her merchants (Rev: 18:23). There is no mention of a military.

- If Ancient Rome had been defeated by ten kings, not expecting its demise, shouldn't we know each of the king's names and where they were from?

- All ten kings simultaneously, at an appointed time, destroy the harlot when it is not expected.

- She is the mother of all harlots, or in other words, the greatest deceiver of all.

- Unlike Rome, the mark of the beast comes shortly after the great cities destruction.

- Unlike Rome, the saints were not persecuted for only forty-two months by the man of perdition.

- In Daniel's vision there is no mention of ten toes, assuming they supported the Roman Empire. Toes were included in King Nebuchadnezzar's statue. Daniel's vision of a fourth kingdom mentioned only ten horns, but the toes were excluded.

Revelation 18:17–18, all that are at sea who have traded with the harlot will see the smoke of her destruction. Revelation 18:3 informs us that all nations will drink her wine. This means North Korea, Iran, along with every nation will be involved with the great cities trade. How could every nation or kingdom see her smoke? The smoke from Ancient Rome would have to travel to Egypt, throughout the Mediterranean Sea to inland nations, in all directions. Lands far to the east, including China, traded with this mighty nation. I don't have a good enough imagination to think that it is possible for every sea captain that traded with Ancient Rome would see her smoke, unless this takes place in modern times. Modern media would be the only way to view this event, especially by all the sea captains that have traded with her. There is another reason why Ancient Rome could not represent the harlot. Even after Rome's defeat she never lost the voice of Jesus or followers of him.

"The light of a lamp shall not shine in you anymore, and the voice of bridegroom and bride shall not be heard in you anymore. For your merchants were the great men of the earth, for by your sorcery all the nations were deceived" (Rev. 18:23).

She will no longer have what she had before her destruction (Rev.18:22). In Chapters 17 and 18, we find the harlot, the great city corrupting kings of the world as all nations fornicate with her and share in the great harlot's bed. She deceives the entire world and is the worst of her kind. In the eighteenth chapter we see what this great city really is, a city that deceives and controls the whole world through world trade. The harlot's power comes from her merchants, merchandise and sea captains delivering her goods. She is rich and seductive, sharing her golden cup with all, which is full of sin as it moves from nation to nation until the whole world becomes rich and drunk from her alluring wine.

"Now I saw when the Lamb opened one of the seals; and I heard one of the four living creatures saying with a voice like thunder, "Come and see." V2 And I looked, and behold, a white horse. He who sat on it had a bow; and a crown was given to him, and he went out conquering and to conquer" (Rev. 6:1–2).

The harlot is the only metaphor that relates to the first seal, the white horse and its rider. When its ride is finished the red horse and its rider will replace it and begin to remove peace from the earth. With information collected from three proclaiming angels, once the gospel has been given to the entire world, the harlot, the great city of trade is then destroyed and from there on peace is removed from the earth until the return of our Lord. The harlot connects to the white horse, as both follow the same sequence of events.

Although this wicked city reigns over kings, kingdoms and all nations partake in her sins, apparently she conquers and continues to conquer. Many nations have joined this world trade system and some have been removed or exited. The WTO will continuously be involved in convincing all to join her. In the past, Russia was a global trade partner, but later removed. There will be a constant struggle for world dominance, to be king of the mountain. Even though the WTO is the mightiest trade organization, many that trade with her are defiant to join and miss out on the many benefits that are offered. Russia was a G-8 (a Global 8 trade partner) and later became non-compliant to a one world trade system that would also, to an extent, control them. There are many variants to why all nations are not fully engaged with this system. New York City, the WTO, the IMF, Wall Street, and many other economic powers do not and will not appeal to all. In 2017 Russia's President Putin proclaimed that the United States will never rule the world and this was referring to trade. So, trade marches on and continues to conquer as this relates to the first seal, the white horse. When this great city is destroyed a new world order will then rise and make all bow to a great lie. Many will take a mark on the right hand or forehead to show allegiance to Satan's kingdom. Death will come to most that will not accept the mark. Revelation's three proclaiming angels support this foundation. The third angel proclaims "the great tribulation" and blessed are the ones that do not join with this kingdom of evil, which includes Satan and his prophet. To most, by rejecting evil, death is unavoidable.

As we study this woman, this whore, we come to the realization that there is nothing pointing to any kind of military or religious basis. Although, believers do live in the city and are called out before it is destroyed (Rev. 18:4). Non-believers will not hear or believe in God's warning to leave the city. The harlot pertains to riches, seduction, deceit, greed, and world control through trade and reigns over all kings and kingdoms. She is also supported by Leviathan's seven heads or kingdoms (Rev17:3). This scarlet beast represents evil, including its ten horns (kings) and all have blasphemous names. Every kingdom that has come against Israel has blasphemed God. This is the same beast that appears in Revelation, Chapters 12, 13 and 17, and connects with many books throughout the Bible. The great city is portrayed as being very rich, dressed in purple and scarlet with gold and precious pearls. She holds in her hand a golden cup, "with whom the kings of the earth commit fornication, and the inhabitants of earth were made drunk with the wine of her fornication" (Rev. 17:2). This golden cup must be very tempting to entice all nations and kings to partake of her wine, her riches; even to the ones that want to destroy her. You could say that the nations are deceived into believing that trading with this great city is of great benefit to them. Do they understand that this whore's cup is full of deceit and abominations? Isn't it ironic that the harlot that deceives the world also deceives herself? She sits as queen claiming that she alone has built this magnificent city and answers to no one. Yet, she will not see her looming destruction, believing she is so loved because of sharing her wealth as no one would have a reason to destroy her (Rev. 18:7). She sleeps with any that gives her pleasure and power. All nations become rich because of her mighty merchants and through the abundance of her luxury.

The United States of America is a last stronghold of Christianity. In past decades, this nation has spread her great eagle's wings and entered many countries in the name of human rights. Some entries have had military action attached to them. Many past U.S. presidents have released the white dove, hoping the world will accept our peace. Yet many have tried to kill this offer as the United States goes out as a savior to the world, in the name of democracy. We now see a new strategy. In the name of trade, peace is being attained. The WTO is winning peace and control through its trade. This organization can conquer without firing a shot. Without the blessings of the Middle East and China, man will not complete his mission to dominate the world through trade. I do not believe the one sitting on this white horse is the Antichrist, rather the harlot of Revelation. However, the one sitting on the red horse probably is Satan the Destroyer, for the blood of men shall flow like rivers. A false religion takes peace from the white horse.

"And the woman whom you saw is that great city which reigns over the kings of the earth" (Rev. 17:18).

Through trade, this city is controlling the kings of the world. Why would God want to destroy this system?

"For your merchants were the great men of the earth, for by your sorcery all the nations were deceived" (Rev. 18:23).

This great city offers riches and abominations to any who share in her golden cup as she makes all nations drunk, yet rich. Eventually, Leviathan's ten horns, the eighth and last kingdom, will be used by Satan to destroy this great city and then convince the world to come against the saints in the hope of conquering God's throne.

Leviathan's heads are evil and according to Rev. 17:9, they support the greatest illusion that has ever been conceived. Although this harlot is supported by the heads of this sea serpent, she is no better than the beast she rides. She is evil, and with the help of the rich and powerful she rules the earth through trade and deceives all at the same time. The horns are another matter and have everything to do with ushering in the apocalypse.

Revelation 17:5

And on her forehead a name was written

Why the Hate for Capitalism and Democracy?

September 11, 2001 sent a shock wave throughout the world with the loss of the World Trade Buildings. Bin Laden hated the economic cohesion that the World Trade Organization (WTO) produced. He proclaimed that the West, the devil, was controlling and deceiving the world through trade and Allah says it has to be destroyed. To this day

New York City is the number one city targeted to be nuked!

With a collection of scripture referring to the last great deceiving city, it is without a doubt paralleling today's trade structure. There has never been a system or organization that has obtained so much power, for she is spread throughout the world and sits on many waters.

"Then he said to me, "The waters which you saw, where the harlot sits, are peoples, multitudes, nations and tongues" (Rev. 17:15).

The harlot, the great city, is supported by many nations and all nations are deceived through her deceiving sorceries. Keep in mind how close the prophecy of the gospel is to being fulfilled, being given to all dialects, possibly within this decade or a few years beyond. The fulfillment of Revelation's great city now parallels that of New York City.

"I saw the woman, drunk with the blood of the saints and with the blood of the martyrs of Jesus. And when I saw her, I marveled with great amazement" (Rev. 17:6).

Blood, according to Greek translation means "blood or kindred." I believe it can be translated either way, informing us that Mystery Babylon is drunk with the kindred or blood of the saints that live within her. This could very easily be talking about the Jews that live in the great city, as the Jewish population is very large. Everyone of Jewish blood relates back to Abraham, Isaac and Jacob. God's saints (believers) are called out before it is destroyed.

"And I heard another voice from heaven saying "Come out of her, my people, lest you share in her sins, and lest you receive of her plagues" (Rev. 18:4). "And in her was found the blood of the prophets and saints, and of all who were slain on the earth" (Rev. 18:24).

This verse is informing us that besides the saints, all nationalities of the world are in this great city and this would point toward the United Nations sitting in New York City. There is a very strong warning, to those who will not respond to God's call to leave this city before it is consumed by fire. Understand that God is only trying to call out his saints and not the ungodly, for they will not adhere to his warning. This is as close to a repeat of Sodom and Gomorrah as one can get. How will God call his saints out of the great city before he destroys it? Possibly no different than the interpretation that I have presented. If the Jewish race and others open their hearts to the gospel they would be able to believe the revelation that Jesus gave to the apostle John. By understanding the writings of Daniel and John, they could save themselves from a cruel way of dying and possibly lead many to the true Lord, who is the one that gave us these revelations.

Birth of a Colossal Financial System

In 1776, a secret society became known as the "Bavarian Illuminati." Many held high positions, such as politicians and many were connected to finance and banking. Their goal was to rule the world by a few special elect. They became a threat, even to the Roman Catholic Church. Their organization was later banned and some were imprisoned. Years later many claimed that these powerful people went underground and carried on to dominate world affairs. Today, conspiracies thrive as suspicion points to a group now known as the "Illuminati." I believe this organization now wears a new face and that is; The World Trade Organization.

"And on her forehead a name was written: MYSTERY, BABYLON THE GREAT, THE MOTHER OF HARLOTS AND OF THE ABOMINATIONS OF THE EARTH." (Rev. 17:5)

The word "Babylon" in the Old Testament means to confuse or confound. The New Testament refers the name to abomination, idolatry and disgust. It is just about a joke when this translation is considered in relation to Wall Street and the World Trade Organization. In late fall of 2008, the world found that the base of world finance was flawed. Along with this came an infestation of deceit and corruption. Mass confusion set in as the wealth of the world began to evaporate at an alarming rate with drunken investors running the show. This fits perfectly with Revelation 17:6, and I have not yet touched the United States political system.

Is this great cities agenda veiled, so no one except those who control the trade of the world, see the deceit and sin that is found in her? Is this whore embracing her enemy, as she sells her security only to increase her wealth and power? Is she twisting the truth by offering her golden cup that is full of abominations to any who chooses to drink of it and become rich? There are several identifications in the Bible referring to the word "*woman.*" One of these is Israel, one that is pure as another identifies the nation as a harlot. Even Jerusalem has played a whore, sinful and evil. "The Mother of Harlots" refers to the most wicked whore of all time. Jerusalem has been claimed to be this harlot, but she is not a trade city, so it cannot be considered. It is written that a great city will rule over the kings of the world! You cannot get away from the fact that New York City contains the most powerful financial system ever devised by man. It is a global system and without a doubt, controls world finance. To this date this organization controls over ninety percent of international trade.

1 Timothy 6:10

"For the love of money is a root of all *kinds* of evil, for which some have strayed from the faith in their greediness, and pierced themselves through with many sorrows."

Leviathan, with its evil, embraces this whore, yet it will destroy her.

It is fascinating that our current trade system is controlled by the Global 7 (G7) and is entwined with the World Trade Organization. Any nation that is to be included has to adhere to this system's extremely strict rules. This organization includes Canada, France, Germany, Italy, Japan, the United Kingdom and the United States and is the foundation of the WTO, for it sits on many waters.

"Then one of the seven angels who had the seven bowls came and talked with me, saying to me, "Come, I will show you the judgment of the great harlot who sits on many waters," (Rev. 17:1). "Then he said to me, "The waters which you saw, where the harlot sits, are peoples, multitudes, nations and tongues" (Rev. 17:15).

The harlot is supported by a scarlet blasphemous beast with seven heads with blasphemous names. Power, pride and evil is the main theme that connects to Leviathan. The harlot does not care who she sleeps with and is the queen of deceivers. She is supported by Leviathan's heads, but not the horns as they will destroy her. After that event, two of Leviathan's heads, the bear and leopard will dominate the world through the power of Leviathan's ten horns.

Fifty years ago just about everyone in the United States would have felt rather nauseous to what is taking place; a society that compares to prophecy written by the apostle John. New York City, the world's great financial city, is overwhelming liberal, openly embracing homosexuals and increasingly hating Christianity. As written, this city is a place of demons and every foul spirit. A world that once was in awe of this great city and nation cannot figure out what kind of spirit America now lives under, having an acceptance of lying politicians, judges, even unethical presidents that can be voted in more than once. This has replaced nobility and the love for righteousness. I'm not going to give every verse on prophecy, but we are told that the love of many will wax cold. We are becoming so immune to televised sex, violence, drugs, corruption, profanity, nudity and death. Our emotions are becoming numb to all this. Lying is now a part of our political system and surprisingly is accepted by many. Our great leaders carry on without a hint of awareness to what is about to unfold, regarding biblical prophecy. We now have terrorist hiding within this country and one day, be it five, ten or fifteen years, they will be called upon to do what they were trained for, and that is to bring the United Stated down with every imaginable tool possible, especially with the use of nuclear weapons.

New York has within her many powerful, influential and political economic organizations like the United Nations, the WTO, the powerful International Monetary Fund (IMF) and many other groups that endorse an organized world and would like to have all world powers covered under one umbrella. This relates to Revelation's harlot, as she sells herself to the world with the help of her merchants and reigns over kings and kingdoms. In this respect it makes her think she is secure, so loved that no one would dare to destroy her (Rev. 18:7).

Why has our government been giving away our jobs? Selling or giving them to any nation that wishes to trade with us. Over the last decade bankruptcies have busted through the roof with thousands losing their homes and livelihoods. Honest, hard-working people in this country have been misled and sacrificed in the name of global occupation.

During the nineties the Clinton administration allowed investments that were so overrated. Most believed that they could not lose. Investing in the stock market became like playing a pyramid scheme. No one wanted to question the validity of their purchase as long as it gained value. Investors in their twenties were quickly becoming millionaires, buying luxury items like boats, homes and other expensive acquisitions that before had been unreachable. Then there was Alan Greenspan, the most powerful chairman of the Federal Reserve. He gave a comforting report that the United States would see an incline in the job market, while encouraging risky lending practices. However, the market stayed sluggish. He then warned Congress not to create trade barriers so, of course, jobs continued to be transferred to foreign governments. This was not very good news for those who wanted to keep jobs from leaving America, along with its sovereignty and a high standard of living. God is patient but just. Are those who are connected to world economics managing to be caught in their own snare, their own net? Luke 21:34–38 reveals that their own deceit will bring them tumbling down. He destroyed Sodom and Gomorrah and many other kingdoms that were entwined with evil. Don't think he won't do the same to the greatest financial system ever devised by man, all directed from one city, New York.

In 1993, Ross Perot, a successful businessman and presidential candidate, warned America to resist President Clinton from signing NAFTA, the North American Free Trade Agreement. Americans would lose their jobs, mainly to Mexico. On January 1, 1994, President Clinton signed this agreement under the noses of mainly a misguided nation, and then it happened again. On January 1, 1995, came the birth of the WTO, the World Trade Organization. This system came to be with the help of the WTCA, the World Trade Center Association. The loss of American jobs sent shockwaves through the nation. With NAFTA silently merging into the WTO, the United States manufacturing slowly drifted and declined. By the time the U.S. workers realized what had taken place, it was too late. The economic beast was devouring the world. With the middle class taking the brunt of the decline as the ultra-wealthy increased their wealth and power. Top executives in U.S. made decisions to purchase from the outside, only if the price was right. There was no way out for the average American. Many family-owned businesses have been blessed with loyal workers. However, this means nothing to today's management which is only interested in future profits.

The U.S. Corporate Tax was also a tool to drive industry out of this country. By doing so the WTO increased its power as it quickly expanded to other countries. This again softened America by importing cheaper goods. The game has been to eliminate workers that have built successful businesses and head for foreign countries that will make them wealthier. This was all directed by the most powerful organization conceived by mankind.

Even if jobs return, only the higher technical ones will benefit some Americans, but the average worker will not see a great increase as more profits continue to flow to the board of directors. Globalization of economics under one roof is the agenda, all directed by a few powerful elite, having multitudes reacting to their demands. Just think of the power this organization holds over the world. The WTO is also manipulating an ongoing economic war. This great city will hold to its leadership. All nations will eventually drink of her golden cup and the WTO enables this. The last count of countries that have joined the WTO since July 2016 was 164, and this is from a total of 195. Over three quarters of the world's nations have joined this global power and over ninety percent of international trade is now controlled by it. A key prophecy is being fulfilled and most that are living today will see this economic whore conquer the world through economics.

Although Geneva, Switzerland is the other half of the WTO, we have plainly seen that in the fall of 2008, Wall Street is the place that not only affects world trade but also finance. These actions shook the core of the world financial system. From the Global 7 to world trade organizations, we are left with a few powerful rich elite controlling billions of people, all are connected through trade.

Is it a coincidence that GATT (General Agreement on Tariffs and Trade) formed in 1947, a forerunner of what will become the WTO, an organization that parallels the prophesied harlot and the prophecy of the Jews to becoming a state? The harlot and the State of Israel were conceived, virtually in the same year. Keep in mind when Leviathan rises up out of the bottomless pit (Rev. 17:7-8), the unsaved will marvel and chase after this beast and yet it supports the harlot until Leviathan's horns are given authority to destroy the great city. Even the apostle John was deceived or taken in by what he was shown.

"May those curse it who curse the day, Those who are ready to arouse Leviathan" (Job 3:8).

After studying this intriguing metaphor, the realization is that this sea beast has once again been called upon to come against Israel, especially by her Arab neighbors. Approaching two thousand years of dormancy, an ancient land that the Jews once occupied now begins to sprout young leaves (Matt.24:32), and this was prophesied with the return of God's chosen to create the new State of Israel. Besides Israel's newly acquired technology and increase in wealth, great hatred is beginning to build to destroy her.

It is astounding that with the birth of this economic world trade system, two prophecies are now converging! The entire world is about to receive the gospel and the harlot is a city controlling the nations through her trade.

Today, as expressed in the Book of Daniel, the bear and leopard are also becoming an increasingly larger part of this prophesied event that will eventually lead to a combined kingdom. The lion, bear and leopard, along with Satan, his prophet and the dreaded ten horns will be the new kingdom. These beasts will dominate and strip the lion in Daniel 7, of its great eagle wings and this is all brought on by Leviathan's horns.

With the connection of Revelation's thirteenth chapter through the nineteenth, it becomes clear that the sea beast Leviathan will be called upon to destroy not only Israel but also the harlot, the great city of trade.

The call for the death of America has not ceased. Jubilation constantly vibrates in the minds of terrorists, remembering the destruction of the World Trade Buildings. One day an entire city will collapse in fire and peace through trade will no longer prevail. For the great cities destruction comes at a time that is not foreseen. Cohesion of nations through trade will no longer exist as the fiery red horse and horseman begin their hellish ride.

Should You Trade within this Great Cities System?

There has been trade between countries for thousands of years, so what would be the problem with trading in this newly established global trade system? Take a serious look at what has been considered "normal trade" and trade of the World Trade Organization. One would have to be blind not to see what has been and what is currently being done. The United States, with its powerful trade leaders, have and are being deceived by a few powerful elite. For many years the U.S. has been at the top in innovation, finance, manufacturing, outright wealth and so forth. No other country has done what we have accomplished. To this day many still do not get it as America continues to sell herself off to the world. The master plan has been masterfully executed. Security of our children has been questioned as American jobs and technology has been transferred to foreign countries. Even segments of our military are now produced in countries that continue to be a direct enemy. We have seen many corporations in the United States selling themselves to countries like China for the sake of profits and some believe this makes us more secure. We send our companies to do business in parts of the world that completely hate us and someday they could use our own technology to destroy us. After finishing this chapter, ask yourself a question: Would you like to transfer or start your business in China or any other country that is increasingly becoming belligerent towards the United States and also, Christianity? Why do you think the very elite, the utmost of economic leaders are handing the golden cup to anyone who will drink from it, or any country that wants to trade through this system? It's not only for greed and the love of money, as it is also for the power to control.

"The light of a lamp shall not shine in you anymore, and the voice of bridegroom and bride shall not be heard in you anymore. For your merchants were the great men of the earth, for by your sorcery all the nations were deceived. V24 And in her was found the blood of the prophets and saints, and of all who were slain on the earth" (Rev. 18:23–24).

This city will fall so hard that not even a light will shine in her anymore. Her devastation will be complete and continue forever. No longer will the voice of Christianity be heard in this city anymore, ever!

Apparently, this city presents the word of God, having believers in it before its total destruction. The harlot spreads deceit with the help of her merchants. Trade is a veil that covers a monstrous lie, a great delusion which leads to unrivaled power.

"And the woman whom you saw is that great city which reigns over the kings of the earth" (Rev. 17:18).

This global system could eventually control how you live, even your spiritual beliefs. Today, this book or the book of Revelation does not conform to the peace and safety of the world. I believe it will not be long before I am restricted from writing a book like this!

The components of New York City parallel Revelation's harlot. Anyone that uses this platform and partners with this system is in fornication with her. Are you now part of her? Give to Caesar what is Caesar's, but do not embrace a sorcery that our government now fully supports; a system that has eroded our sovereignty. At this moment this organization tolerates any religion, as long as it does not interfere with its trade.

Many proclaim there will be no peace on earth until our Lord returns to reclaim it. Many non-Christians believe there will be peace on earth that comes only through trade and this leads to no more wars. Nation will coexist with nation. Indifferences will be put aside for the sake of economics, unity and peace. Religions will blend together until they are as one. Controversy of faith will disappear as this global unity grows and matures. Currently, there is a passionate move by those who have come to their senses. They now understand the power of this new trade and how Americans have been sold a bill of goods. They have been deceived and they know it. It is no secret that the tentacles of Wall Street have sunk deeply into the sides of lady liberty, controlling her fate. Indeed, you can get rich investing into other countries. As prophesied, the harlot will continue to reign until its destruction. It seems this country has put itself up for sale and those investing in this system will continue to become wealthier. This global setup has been successful, and for the skilled U. S. worker, terrible hardships have been set in place.

It now appears that there is a new direction, mainly because of a new president. President Donald J. Trump has exposed a large amount of corruption that has infiltrated our government and its trade system. I cannot disagree. What I am intrigued to find; will he lead our country to global truth that will be so transparent that the entire world will come to understand the inner workings of the goal that the WTO has in store? According to scripture the answer is no. The city will continue to deceive to its end. There is a strong possibility that this president could direct this global organization to a pinnacle that has not yet been imagined and one day this great trade city will declare herself as queen, consumed with the belief that no one would dare to destroy her.

"There the ships sail about; *There* is that Leviathan Which You have made to play there" (Ps. 104:26).

This verse connects to the harlot, with her merchants and sea captains delivering her merchandise. Figuratively, this sea beast waits below, passing time; why? The end of this verse is extremely intriguing, "there is that Leviathan which You have made to play there." Mankind has created the harlot, representing trade, greed, pride, control and evil and unknowingly has invited Leviathan's ten horns to partake in her death, mixing evil with evil. Figuratively, when this sea beast rises up, it will strike and the harlot falls to her death.

"In the measure that she glorified herself and lived luxuriously, in the same measure give her torment and sorrow; for she says in her heart, 'I sit as queen, and am no widow, and will not see sorrow.' V8 Therefore her plagues will come in one day – death and mourning and famine. And she will be utterly burned with fire, for strong is the Lord God who judges her (Rev. 18:7-8). "Rejoice over her, O heaven, and *you* holy apostles and prophets, for God has avenged you on her!" (Rev. 18:20).

The harlot glorifies herself and will not give God or any other credit or praise for her success.

Summary of the Harlot, Mystery Babylon, the Great Trade City

Ancient Babylon was known as a great trade city. Mystery Babylon, the harlot of Revelation is also known as a great trade city. Both are said to sit on many waters. This includes peoples, multitudes, nations and tongues (Rev. 17:15).

- Revelation's Babylon has the voice of the bridegroom (Jesus) and his bride (Christians) within her (Rev. 18:23), unlike Ancient Babylon. This ancient city never had the voice of the bridegroom or Christianity.

- She rules over kings through trade, not by the military (Rev. 18:9–15).

- She is supported by the heads of Leviathan, even though its ten horns will destroy the great city, Mystery Babylon (Rev. 17:9).

- She has every nationality living in her, including the blood or kindred of the prophets (Rev. 18:24).

- She has the blood of the martyrs, followers of Jesus that live in Mystery Babylon; both Jew and Gentile (Rev. 17:6).

- She sits as a queen and sees no sorrow. She does not see her imminent destruction, unlike Ancient Babylon or Rome (Rev. 18:7).

- She is the mother of all harlots (Rev. 17:5).

- She rules over all the kings of the world (Rev. 17:18).
- She is hated by Leviathan's ten horns. The ten kings that have no kingdom (Rev. 17:12–160).
- She is hated by God (Rev. 18:20).
- She sells bodies and souls of men (Rev. 18:13).
- All nations of the world trade with the harlot (Rev. 18:3).
- God hates the ten kings (Leviathan's ten horns) yet he gives them authority to burn the great city, evil against evil (Rev. 17:13–14, 17:16).
- When the great city burns, heaven will rejoice (Rev. 18:20).
- After the harlot is destroyed the merchants of the world have no one to trade with. As there is no one to control trade, world economics will collapse (Rev. 18:9–19).
- The apocalypse begins with the burning of the great city. Then the mark of the beast comes, along with Daniel's little horn, Satan (Rev. 14:9).

If any claim that Ancient Rome is the great trade city of Revelation, then one would also have to understand that at the very end of Rome's dominance she did not sit in her own security. This also refers to Ancient Babylon. Unlike both cities, the latter day harlot believes she is secure and will not be destroyed.

Is There Time for Another Great Trade City to Rise?

It is utterly important to understand the message of Revelation's fourteenth chapter with three angels proclaiming to the world. Since the time of Christ, we have been living in the era of the first proclaiming angel. With the rebirth of Israel in 1948, that generation, (Matt. 24:32-35), or what is left of it, will go through the great tribulation. Time is running out and that leaves little room for another city to rise and replace New York as the center of world trade. A city already exists that compares to Revelation's great city, Mystery Babylon.

Nobody knows the day or hour, but within the last decades this process of delivering the gospel has increased enormously. God has declared that he will not be slack with those that hate him, and this points to the completion of the gospel delivered to all tongues, peoples, nations and tribes, in all dialects. The destruction of the harlot could take place immediately after this event. Keep in mind that Matthew 24 declares that the generation of 1948 will experience the great tribulation. Many will not pass away before all these unsurpassed events against mankind unfold. This is my generation and I am nearing seventy years.

With the destruction of this great city, peace is then taken from mankind. The great tribulation then begins, along with judgment on professing believers (Rev. 20:4-6). Once the white horse of the apocalypse has been removed (Rev. 6: 2-4), the red horse will begin its journey of death. Then the false prophet's mark will be required on the forehead or right hand on every soul on earth. This mark represents any that have fallen to the beast and the false prophet that embraces Satan's lie. This happens at the end of the Gentile rule. "For her sins have reached to heaven, and God has remembered her iniquities, V6 Render to her just as she rendered to you, and repay her double according to her works; in the cup which she has mixed, mix double for her" (Rev. 18:5-6).

Chapter 10

Common Threads of Two Cities

Why would the apostle John refer to Babylon in the book of Revelation? We are informed that this city would never rise again (Jer. 50:39, 51:26). Why write a futuristic book that includes a great trade city that has already been destroyed and with such detail? Or was John shown a vision of a new Babylon, a new city that will be warned and prophesied to fall? Mysteriously, the apostle John's great city named Mystery Babylon overlaps and relates to earlier writings; two cities that are connected by the same threads and will have the same fate. Unlike the ancient city of Babylon, there is another city sharing the same traits but it will not linger on after it is attacked. In one day, at an appointed time, it will be utterly destroyed in fire and its smoke will rise forever. The comparison is staggering. I love the foundation of my country, but we are in very deep trouble as there is an urgency to comprehend this great whore.

Scripture that should concern any that research eschatology.

- Babylon was a splendid city to which all nations came (Dan. 3:7). This city was known as a great trade city.

- All flesh was fed from it (Dan. 4:12). Nebuchadnezzar's rule of Babylon would dominate the earth (Dan. 4:22). God declared

Babylon would be repaid according to her work because this city had been proud against the Lord.

- "Babylon *was* a golden cup in the Lord's hand, that made all the earth drunk. The nations drank her wine; Therefore the nations are deranged" (Jer. 51:7).

- "O, you who dwell by many waters, Abundant in treasures, Your end has come, The measure of your covetousness" (Jer. 51:13).

- "And the land will tremble and sorrow; For every purpose of the Lord shall be performed against Babylon, To make the land of Babylon a desolation without inhabitant" (Jer. 51:29).

- "Babylon shall become a heap, A dwelling place for jackals, An astonishment and a hissing, Without an inhabitant" (Jer. 51:37).

- "My people, go out of the midst of her! And let everyone deliver himself from the fierce anger of the Lord" (Jer. 51:45).

- "Then the heavens and the earth and all that *is* in them Shall sing joyously over Babylon; For the plunderers shall come to her from the north," says the Lord" (Jer. 51:48).

- "Sit in silence, and go into darkness, O daughter of the Chaldeans; For you shall no longer be called The Lady of Kingdoms. V6 I was angry with My people; I have profaned My inheritance, And given them into your hand. You showed them no mercy; On the elderly you laid your yoke very heavily. V7 And you said, 'I shall be a lady forever,' So that you did not take these *things* to heart, Nor remember the latter end of them. V8 Therefore hear this now*, you who are* given to pleasures, Who dwell securely, Who say in your heart, 'I am, and *there is* no one else besides me; I shall not sit *as* a widow, Nor shall I know the loss of children';" (Isa. 47:5–8).

The first main blow that came to Babylon shortly after Nebuchadnezzar's death in 539 BC was by Gobryas, one of Cyrus's generals. The city then began its decline. Isaiah wrote about Babylon, describing how this great city and its leaders corrupted and mislead the nations that came to her. God used this powerful nation to punish Judah, a portion of his chosen people. The Babylonians so severely mistreated the Jews that God sent the Persians in to defeat this proud and powerful kingdom. What is absolutely astounding; *Ancient Persia will eventually become the new Persia and will come against a new city, a new Mystery Babylon.* I fully believe this great city of trade, which geographically sits on the other side of the world, is New York City. In this new city there is no mention of bondage pertaining to the Jews, which is just the opposite with historical Babylon. God calls his saints out of this great city before it is consumed by fire. I believe, many will stay because of the desire, passion, greed and love for what this city represents. Many will continue to put their faith in this grandest of schemes, controlling and deceiving the world through trade (Rev. 18:13–15).

I see two Babylons; one is historical and said never to rise again, the other is Mystery Babylon, which is set in the future, beyond the former. This time, the new city lies in a different geographical location and it is somewhat hard to distinguish from the former. It is written that it will be a land of desolation without inhabitant, which did not happen to Ancient Babylon, at least not after it was invaded by the Persians. It is also very important to understand that historical Ancient Babylon never had the voice of Jesus, the bridegroom, unlike Mystery Babylon, the great city of trade (Rev.18:23). This is one of the mysteries of the second and last Babylon. I believe Isaiah's and Jeremiah's writings overlap both kingdoms. One city existed at the time of their writings and the other was to be in the future. Both share the same traits and to a point; the same fate. Revelation's nineteenth chapter proclaims "Alleluia! Salvation and glory and honor and power *belong* to the Lord our God!" (Rev. 19:1). Heaven rejoices over the harlots' destruction.

Comparison of Both Cities

From the time of Jeremiah, Isaiah, Daniel, the apostle John, along with other prophets, Babylon has been infused in their writings. Especially, with the connection of the ten horns, described by Daniel and John. These horns or kings will eventually destroy the harlot, the great city of trade.

After the fall of Ancient Babylon, hundreds of years pass. In time, the Romans exiled John to the island of Patmos where he wrote about

Mystery Babylon. Why would John even consider writing about this ancient kingdom, as it had been destroyed hundreds of years earlier and prophesied never to rise again? After Revelation's fourth chapter John writes on prophesy throughout the rest of his book, events pertaining to the future. My premise: he is writing about a new city, a new Babylon, a great city that has an enigma attached to it. A city that will be ruled by powerful people and deceive the world through the power of trade. This deceit by Mystery Babylon of Revelation 17 and 18 has the same face as that of the former Babylon. Both kingdoms have golden cups full of wine, causing the nations to become drunk. The wine is alluring, deceiving the world because of the riches she creates. Greed, control and the love for power drives the harlot to her pinnacle and every nation will share in her abominations. Both cities proclaim to see no sorrow and lead the world astray. Both proclaim they will not sit as a widow, both are proud and sit as a queen. Both proclaim security and yet they are defeated in one day. One survives and continues for a number of years, the other quickly collapses in its own ashes. Ancient Babylon slowly crumbled. Mystery Babylon will end in one day. Angels in heaven sing about its destruction. Revelation 17:5 refers to this last great trade city as "MYSTERY, BABYLON THE GREAT, THE MOTHER OF HARLOTS AND OF THE ABOMINATIONS OF THE EARTH."

"Then he said to me, "The waters which you saw, where the harlot sits, are peoples, multitudes, nations, and tongues. V16 And the ten horns which you saw on the beast, these will hate the harlot, make her desolate and naked, eat her flesh and burn her with fire. V17 For God has put it into their hearts to fulfill His purpose, to be of one mind, and to give their kingdom to the beast, until the words of God are fulfilled. V18 And the woman whom you saw is that great city which reigns over the kings of the earth" (Rev. 17:15–18).

Revelation's harlot will deceive beyond any scheme of man. The ones who control this great city are powerful, even her great merchants of the earth are deceived. She is the queen of liars and deceivers! There are two Babylons. One is historical, which would be Ancient Babylon, and proclaimed not to rise again. The other is Mystery Babylon, a great city that exists at this very day! A crucial difference: Ancient Babylon was defeated by the Persians, but the city continued on. When Revelation's great city, Mystery Babylon, is attacked and burned by ten kings, it takes place in one day, at an appointed time she will be destroyed as her smoke shall rise forever and ever (Rev. 19:1-3).

We are informed through Revelation 18:15-17, the merchants and sea captains stand far off and do not dare come near her, as this could be contributed to a nuclear event.

Key Verses Connecting Ancient Babylon to Revelation's Mystery Babylon

- Babylon was a splendid city to which all people, nations and languages came (Dan. 3:7).
- "Then he said to me, "The waters which you saw, where the harlot sits, are peoples, multitudes, nations and tongues" (Rev. 17:15).
- Nebuchadnezzar's dream: "all flesh was fed from it" (Dan. 4:12).
- "And the woman whom you saw is that great city which reigns over the kings of the earth" (Rev. 17:18).
- "Babylon *was* a golden cup in the Lord's hand, That made all the earth drunk. The nations drank her wine; Therefore the nations are deranged" (Jer. 51:7).
- "For all the nations have drunk of the wine of the wrath of her fornication, the kings of the earth have committed fornication with her, and the merchants of the earth have become rich through the abundance of her luxury" (Rev. 18:3).
- "O you who dwell by many waters, Abundant in treasures, Your end has come, The measure of your covetousness" (Jer. 51:13).
- "And the land will tremble and sorrow; For every purpose of the Lord shall be performed against Babylon, To make the land of Babylon a desolation without inhabitant" (Jer. 51:29).
- "And the ten horns which you saw on the beast, these will hate the harlot, make her desolate and naked, eat her flesh and burn her

with fire" (Rev. 17:16). "The kings of the earth who committed fornication and lived luxuriously with her will weep and lament for her, when they see the smoke of her burning" (Rev. 18:9).

- "Babylon shall become a heap, A dwelling place for jackals, An astonishment and a hissing, Without an inhabitant" (Jer. 51:37).

- "And he cried mightily with a loud voice, saying, "Babylon the great is fallen, is fallen, and has become a dwelling place of demons, a prison for every foul spirit, and a cage for every unclean and hated bird!" (Rev. 18:2)

- "Then the heavens and the earth and all that *is* in them Shall sing joyously over Babylon; For the plunderers shall come to her from the north," says the Lord. V49 As Babylon *has caused* the slain of Israel to fall, so at Babylon the slain of all the earth shall fall" (Jer. 51:48-49).

- "In the measure that she glorified herself and lived luxuriously, in the same measure give her torment and sorrow; for she says in her heart, 'I sit as queen, and am no widow, and will not see sorrow. V8 "Therefore her plagues will come in one day – death and mourning and famine. And she will be utterly burned with fire, for strong *is* the Lord God who judges her" (Rev. 18:7-8). "Rejoice over her, O heaven, and *you* holy apostles and prophets, for God has avenged you on her!" (Rev. 18:20).

- "Sit in silence, and go into darkness, O daughter of the Chaldeans; For you shall no longer be called The Lady of Kingdoms. V6 I was angry with My people; I have profaned My inheritance, And given them into your hand. You showed them no mercy; On the elderly you laid your yoke very heavily. V7 And you said, 'I shall be a lady forever,' So that you did not take these *things* to heart, Nor remember the latter end of them. "V8 Therefore hear this now, *you who* are given to pleasures, who dwell securely, Who say in your heart, 'I *am*, and *there is* no one else besides me; I shall not sit *as* a widow, Nor shall I know the loss of children'; V9 But these two *things* shall come to you. In a moment, in one day: The loss of children, and widowhood, They shall come on you in their fullness Because of the multitude of your sorceries, For the great abundance of your enchantments"

(Isa. 47:5–9). Could the loss of children connect to the killing of new and unborn babies?

- "And the land will tremble and sorrow; For every purpose of the Lord shall be performed against Babylon, To make the land of Babylon a desolation without inhabitant" (Jer. 51:29).

- "After these things I heard a loud voice of a great multitude in heaven, saying, "Alleluia! Salvation and glory and honor and power *belong* to the Lord our God! V2 For true and righteous *are* His judgments, because He has judged the great harlot who corrupted the earth with her fornication; and He has avenged on her the blood of his servants *shed* by her." V3 Again they said, "Alleluia! Her smoke rises up forever and ever!" (Rev. 19:1-3).

In this last verse, Mystery Babylon's smoke rises forever and ever and cannot relate to Ancient Babylon as this city eventually became desolate many years after the Persian invasion. Revelation 18:7-8 again separates the two cities. Mystery Babylon is destroyed in one day and her smoke will rise forever and ever. Again, this did not take place with Ancient Babylon which became, for many years, ruled by Persians. Babylon is also named "the daughter of the Chaldeans." In comparing both cities we see striking similarities. Daniel, Chapter 3, describes all of Nebuchadnezzar's subjects bowing to his great image of gold. Wall Street also has the same affect.

"Again they say, "Alleluia! Her smoke rises up forever and ever!" (Rev. 19:3). This verse separates Ancient Babylon from Mystery Babylon. "The light of a lamp shall not shine in you anymore, and the voice of bridegroom and bride shall not be heard in you anymore. For your merchants were the great men of the earth, for by your sorcery all nations were deceived" (Rev. 18:23).

Ancient Babylon never had the voice of the bridegroom or bride, so this kingdom and city has to be omitted from representing the harlot. Rome survived and continued spreading the gospel of the Lord, so it also has to be ruled out. Neither of these ancient kingdoms compare to Mystery Babylon. When this city is destroyed her smoke will rise forever and ever and ever!

"Then the heavens and the earth and all that *is* in them Shall sing joyously over Babylon; For the plunderers shall come to her from the north," says the Lord." V49 As Babylon *has caused* the slain of Israel to fall. So at Babylon the slain of all the earth shall fall." (Jer. 51:48–49).

These two verses relate to Revelation's great city, Rev. 17:6 and Rev.18:24. The main reason for Ancient Babylon's fall; they treated the Jews too severely and Revelation's great city mentions none of this; this city is destroyed because of deceit, pride and evil and also leads the world astray.

Chapter 11

Leviathan's Ten Horns

Understanding the concept of Leviathan also gives up the mystery of how God hid and separated scripture that connects this metaphor. I view this accumulation of information like a tennis match with the ball returned to the opposite court, again and again with information being added, until there was enough knowledge gathered from both sides, then the game ends. Scripture in Daniel connects to Revelation and vice versa. Vital information flows between both books, once a scripture has become enlightened, new information can then be acquired. One book cannot be understood without the other. Clarity heightens as the veil begins to be removed. The mystery has been challenged and eventually revealed.

In many of these next chapters I become very repetitive. Those that have a hard time with metaphors will thank me, others might become annoyed. Leviathan's horns are extremely important to comprehend.

Leviathan's ten horns are attached to a specific head, the second head of seven. This head represents the ancient kingdom of Persia and it connects to Revelation 17:11. The beast that was, is the eighth and of the seven, a kingdom that these horns once ruled (Dan. 7:20), and are the ten kings of the Persian Empire. After the rule of the second head its horns (ten kings) became inactive, dormant. They will not rise again until this beast (kingdom) revives. I fully believe in my lifetime, these horns will once again become active and will be given authority with the beast and then destroy the harlot. Out of Satan's revived kingdom come the rise of these dreaded ten horns (kings) (Dan. 7:24).

The ten horns of Daniel and Revelation have intrigued me beyond any other. Like Daniel, these horns have thrown me into an arena, acquiring knowledge, an understanding to which sometimes I would like to forget. Daniel was a great man of faith, yet he was left without understanding his vision and did not have futuristic writings to lean on, especially the book of Revelation. He was instructed to seal his book (Dan. 12:4). Nebuchadnezzar's dream of four kingdoms would end with the collapse of Rome. John's revelation from Jesus (Rev. 1:1) along with the Book of Daniel, will take us to the very last of days.

In Revelation's tenth chapter, an angel instructed John to eat or consume the words of a little book that was sweet to the taste, yet sour to the stomach. I believe he consumed these words of Daniel and was also instructed not to seal his book, as Revelation is for the time of the end. The seal will be removed as Daniel's book will join with John's writings and then clarity will abound. Both books will be understood before the return of our Lord.

"But you, Daniel, shut up the words, and seal the book until the time of the end; many shall run to and fro, and knowledge shall increase" (Dan. 12:4).

Daniel was told to seal his book until the time of the end (Dan. 12:4). The "end" will be the time of unveiling, a time of understanding. Today, the world moves a thousand times faster than at the time of the old prophets. Knowledge has increased beyond belief. We are at the time of the end.

"You must prophesy again about many peoples, nations, tongues and kings" (Rev.10:11).

In the end times, John's message will be given to all peoples, nations, tongues, tribes and to all dialects. This also includes a prophecy of the "kings" which I believe is referring to Rev. 17:10–12. In the last days, Leviathan's ten horns (kings) will be enlightened as more information accumulates and gives a true sense of this metaphor.

Of Leviathan's seven heads, only one holds the power to begin the apocalypse. This is the second head, representing the revival of the beast that was, Persia. All the old kingdoms that represented Nebuchadnezzar's statue are now history, with the exception of Leviathan's ten horns. Be aware, in Daniel's seventh chapter all four kingdoms (lion, bear, leopard and ten horns) are beyond the life of Daniel. He describes a kingdom (ten horns) that is fully engaged with the beast to which it belongs, which has not yet happened. In Daniel's seventh chapter, the ten horns are fully engaged with the beast that was wounded by the sword and yet revives, partaking in Satan's kingdom that devours the entire earth (Rev.13:3). Daniel, Chapter 7 and Revelation, Chapters 13, 14, 17 and 18 are all futuristic and all connect. These ten horns are first seen in Daniel 7 and would not be understood until the time of the end as they become active with the beast (kingdom) that was.

"The beast that you saw was, and is not, and will ascend out of the bottomless pit and go to perdition. And those who dwell on the earth will marvel, whose names are not written in the Book of Life from the foundation of the world, when they see the beast that was, and is not, and yet is" (Rev. 17:8).

"and the ten horns that *were* on its head, and the other *horn* which came up, before which three fell, namely, that horn which had eyes and a mouth which spoke pompous words, whose appearance *was* greater than his fellows" (Dan. 7:20).

The word "*were*" is italicized and not written in the original Greek or English translation and is not entered in the original source. I view the placement of this word extremely interesting. The ten horns "*were*" links to Revelation's seventeenth chapter; a beast (kingdom) that "was" and will be (Rev. 17:8, 17:12), representing a kingdom that was led by ten kings (Dan. 7:20). A kingdom that God allows to return, being not of the old, rather a new kingdom that has roots connected to its past. This takes place only through the will of God which eventually allows the ten horns to destroy the harlot, the great city, Mystery Babylon (Rev. 13:3, 17:16). A revived kingdom joins with its ancient heritage and is directed by a prophet. Ten kings rise from this kingdom and then the lesser horn (king) rises above the other ten kings, he then kills three, leaving seven. The lion, bear and leopard are living simultaneously at the return of the ten horns. They become consumed and integrated into this new global kingdom to which the false prophet and Satan have given life. This kingdom represents a beast and someday it will destroy global economics and separate the true believer from the false.

Why did this fourth and last kingdom of Daniel's vision upset him? He could not reckon with something that he could not understand. He did not show the emotion of fear, deciphering Nebuchadnezzar's dream, unlike his own. He knew this mystery was far from his grasp. An angel told him to go his way, yet I believe this vision plagued him to his death.

Revelation 17:16

> *"And the ten horns which you saw on the beast, these will hate the harlot, make her desolate and naked, eat her flesh and burn her with fire."*

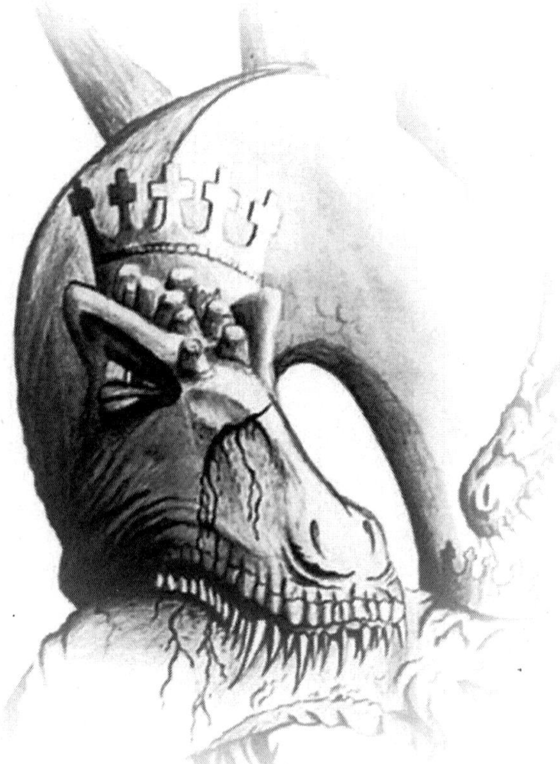

Kings without a Kingdom

"The ten horns which you saw are ten kings who have received no kingdom as yet, but they receive authority for one hour as kings with the beast" (Rev. 17:12).

Are each of these ten kings going to rule their own kingdom or are they just appointed individuals which God gives authority to join with the beast, the kingdom of Satan, and then consume the harlot with fire? The horns are crowned and this gives authority.

Beside Babylonian rule, Daniel lived under the Achaemenid Dynasty and their ten kings ruled in succession. The important difference: the lion, bear, leopard and the ten horns are living simultaneously, all in the same time period and this takes place at the time of the end.

Revelation is often written like a confusing dark riddle, giving information with little or no understanding. Up to this point comprehending the entire book has been anything but possible. Again, without understanding the heads and horns of the sea beast Leviathan, Revelation would never be fully revealed. Let's review important scripture that leads to the reviving of Ancient Persia, the old kingdom that eventually becomes a new kingdom and devours the earth. This is a mystery that I have had a passion to discover. With the information in Daniel 7:23-24, the ten horns rise out of the last evil kingdom that will eventually encapsulate the world. Only after their rise does a lesser king become more dominant.

In Daniel 7:24, when does this powerful king (Satan) kill three of the ten kings (Daniel 7:24)? I can't give the day or year this last king comes to power, but a clue does give the chronological order between the beast, the little horn, and the ten horns. Does the little horn kill three of the ten horns before they destroy the great city, the harlot, and take over the world? The answer is no. As stated in Daniel 7, the ten horns take over the entire earth as described in Revelation 17:12.

"The ten horns which you saw are ten kings who have received no kingdom as yet, but they receive authority for one hour as kings with the beast" (Rev. 17:12).

"And the ten horns which you saw on the beast, these will hate the harlot, make her desolate and naked, eat her flesh and burn her with fire" (Rev. 17:16).

Leviathan's ten horns are not mentioned or seen in Revelation 13:2, yet we are informed in Daniel 7, they take over the entire earth. The point is that all ten horns are intact when they become active with the beast (Rev. 17:12). They sit on one of the heads (Dan. 7:20), one of the kingdoms that is prophesied to return to destroy the harlot, Mystery Babylon, the great city. Only after this are three of the ten kings killed by Satan, the horn of deceit. (Dan. 7:8).

What could conspire? We are informed that at the time of the harlot's demise she is at her pinnacle, believing destruction is not in her future. She will lose the ability to protect herself, possibly by placing those of high security in key places that should have never been allowed or by letting refugees flow into this country, those that have the ability to finish the job, the destruction of New York City. Through God's will, because of his hate towards this city, he will destroy evil with evil with the return of the ten horns (Rev.17:16). We should pray that those saints that live within this city depart before it is too late (Rev. 18:4). There is nothing that any of us can do to prevent her demise, except to try and save souls.

Daniel 7:24 gives order to these events. Out of this prophesied revived kingdom (Rev. 13:3) ten horns (kings) will rise (Dan. 7:23-24) and another king will rise after, for he will be different from the others; for he is Satan. This king also refers to Rev.17:10.

Ancient Persia – Still Breathing

For many years, the ten horns of Daniel and Revelation eluded me. I searched for a kingdom that was ruled by ten horns, ten kings (Dan. 7:20). I was searching for a kingdom that was, and is prophesied to revive.

"And I *saw* one of its heads as if it had been mortally wounded, and his deadly wound was healed. And all the world marveled and followed the beast" (Rev. 13:3).

"The beast that you saw was, and is not, and will ascend out of the bottomless pit and go to perdition. And those who dwell on the earth will marvel, whose names are not written in the Book of Life from the foundation of the world, when they see the beast that was, and is not, and yet is" (Rev. 17:8).

When Leviathan rises up out of the sea, it carries with it all its heads and horns. Leviathan is a beast that "was" and "will be" and also the second head, Ancient Persia, a beast that "was" and "will be."

"And the ten horns which you saw on the beast, these will hate the harlot, make her desolate and naked, eat her flesh and burn her with fire" (Rev. 17:16).

After receiving several books relating to the quest for understanding the ten horns, one stood out and gave me the information which I have long desired. *Ancient Persia,* written by Josef Wiesehofer, placed a dynasty that reigned at the time of Daniel; the Achaemenid. His claim was that ten powerful kings ruled this first dynasty of mighty Persia until Alexander the Great caused it to collapse. Although the kingdom was defeated, it never died, this refers to Rev. 13:3. The Medes and Persians were instruments of God, and were used not only against the Babylonians but also the Jews. The reason that I am concentrating on Ancient Persia more than the other three kingdoms of Nebuchadnezzar's dream, I see this nation (now modern day Iran) being connected through history, to present-day and future prophecy. King Nebuchadnezzar's dream connects the past to the future, with ten powerful kings that connected to the Persian Empire, the Achaemenid. In the last days this kingdom will return and will be given authority to devour the entire world.

In Daniel 7, we can see how disturbed Daniel had become, as his vision was troubling. He did not realize that he was living at the time of these horns, the ten kings. Oblivious to him, these kings would control the first dynasty of the Persian Empire and would one day return to plague the true believers of Jesus. The dynasty consists of Cyrus II, considered the founder of Persia. The count begins with this king. There are additional kings but with fault and legitimacy, they are not considered. Cyrus the Great, Cambyses, Gaumata, Darius I, Xerxes I, Atraxerxes 1, Xerxes II, Darius II, Atraxerxes II, Atraxerxes III, Arses, and Darius III. Xerxes

II ruled for 45 days and was then assassinated, so this king has to be omitted. Gaumata/Bardiya had a problem with the legal right of being king, so the remaining ten kings made up the Achaemenid Dynasty. Ten kings *were* on a head (kingdom) ruling in succession (Dan. 7:20). A beast that was and yet is. Interestingly, the Medes occupied Northern Iraq and for a time ruled over the soon to be Persians. Later, the Persians defeated them. They eventually merged their bloodlines, each having respect for the other. Today there is much fear that Iraq could fall once again into the hands of this ancient kingdom that directly relates to Iran. If U.S. policies don't change, this will absolutely come to be and I could not imagine what kind of power would be produced, especially with an evil prophet that eventually unifies the entire globe. The second kingdom in Nebuchadnezzar's statue is the Persian Empire, which is the second head of Leviathan. Unlike the Roman Empire, modern Rome has none of its features, none of the characteristics that it once projected. Today, Rome is not trying to raise a mighty army of terrorists or spread a religious philosophy that beheads people as described in the twentieth chapter of Revelation. Catholicism is the only string connecting Rome to its ancient past. Today, their leaders do not resemble the ones that led that nation. The only ancient kingdom that resembles what it once was and still connects to its ancient heritage is modern day Iran. Before 1935, this nation was known as the Persian Empire. Iran is the main geographical area in which this empire began and a kingdom that is connected to Daniel 2 and 7, Matthew 24 and Revelation 12, 13, 14, 17 and 18. We see this ancient land still breathing. Ancient Persia intertwines with today's Iran, and to this day many claim to be Persian. The rise of a New Persian Empire is the dream of many Iranians. This is why we should wake up and realize what is about to happen; prophecy is unfolding at a very rapid rate. The leopard of Daniel 7 is about to rise!

There is an article written by Cyrus Kadivar, dated January 25, 2002, from *The Iranian*, titled "We Are Awake." Mr. Kadivar writes about the twenty-five hundred year celebration of Persia. These are some of the highlights:

In AD 1971 there was a party, a celebration in a town that sits in the nation of Iran. This grand event was held under tents to resemble Persian customs. This town is Persepolis, the "City of Persian." It was first built by King Darius and then burned to the ground by Alexander the Great in 331 BC. It now sits isolated in the desert.

The festivity included replicas of ancient costumes and trumpets reconstructed to produce sounds not heard for more than twenty-five centuries. Many dignitaries came, along with hundreds of horses, camels and 1,724 soldiers. Every detail was designed to be Persian. It was such a celebration that the actor Orson Welles came to participate. On October 12, 1971, more than twenty-five hundred years after the Persian conquest of Babylon the celebration began in Pasargadae, at the tomb of Cyrus the Great. The Shah of Iran gave these words on television. "O Cyrus, Great King, King of Kings, Achaemenian King, king of the land of Iran. I, the Shahanshah of Iran offer thee salutations from myself and from my nation. Rest in peace, for we are awake, and we will always stay awake." These events allowed him to show his proud heritage that was connected to Ancient Persia. The people of Iran believe their ancient kingdom still connects and continues to be part of them. We now see the whole picture with the completion of the mystery. One day, along with this ancient kingdom, comes the mark of the beast, prophesied in the book of Revelation. Persia's first dynasty has long disappeared, yet we see an empire that has never died; it has always been. It has never returned to the power as with the first state, the Achaemenid, as their mightiest kings are gone. After Alexander the Great's conquest over this mighty nation it was like receiving a mortal wound and never again did Persia regain recognition that it once had. Although Islam's Persia fought Christians and other kingdoms, winning some major victories, it was never magnified to its former glory, not until God gives the blessing to rise one last time.

As prophesied, there is no trace of the old Babylon, which was the first head (kingdom) of Leviathan. There are those that still proclaim this nation will again rise and dominate the world. However, it is stated that this kingdom would never rise again (Jer. 50:39, 51:26; and 51:39).

An interesting point: Persia is mentioned in the Book of Ezekiel and is connected to the last days with their army coming against Israel, just before the return of Christ. This is considered an end time event. There is also no trace of Alexander's Empire, the third head of Leviathan, nor the four kingdoms that were divided between his four generals. Furthermore, there is no trace of Ancient Rome, the forth head of Leviathan. The kingdom's power is long gone and its sword no longer sustains power. Iran is the only kingdom that claims to be connected to what it once was, the great and mighty Persia. They are connected through prophecy with their ten mighty kings. Once again, they will join to the same kingdom that their ten ancient kings ruled. With the desire of God, the magnificent trade city will be destroyed, along with collapsing world trade.

"Thus he said: 'The fourth beast shall be A fourth kingdom on earth, Which shall be different from all *other* kingdoms, And shall devour the whole earth, Trample it and break it in pieces. V24 The ten horns *are* ten kings *Who* shall arise from this kingdom" (Dan. 7:23-24).

"The beast that was, and is not, is himself also the eighth, and is of the seven, and is going to perdition" (Rev. 17:11).

Daniel, Chapter 7, states the ten horns represent a beast, a kingdom that includes a king. Out of this last kingdom (the eighth) rises Apollyon, Satan. This kingdom tramples and devours the whole earth. A beast includes a king or kings and a kingdom, peoples and armies and a philosophy or foundation on which it stands.

"Then I stood on the sand of the sea. And I saw a beast rising up out of the sea, having seven heads and ten horns, and on his horns ten crowns, and on his heads a blasphemous name. V2. Now the beast that I saw was like a leopard, his feet were like *the feet of* a bear, and his mouth like the mouth of a lion. The dragon gave him his power, his throne, and great authority" (Rev. 13:1–2).

John sees a beast rising up out of the sea with seven heads and ten horns. In the second verse he now focuses on a section of this sea serpent Leviathan. It is a beast that is comprised with a mouth of a lion, feet of a bear and body of a leopard. Daniel 7 enlightens the mystery. This last kingdom will soon encompass the earth and this comes through the power of Leviathan's ten horns. This fourth and last beast consumes the entire earth and will strip the lion of its great eagle's wings and later it will join with Satan's kingdom. The bear becomes the foundation of Satan's foundation.

The ten horns are essential to unraveling Revelation. They *were* on a head, one of Leviathans, (Dan. 7:20). These ten horns (kings) that once ruled an ancient kingdom will return to destroy the great city of trade

(Revelation 17 and 18). Once the gospel is given to all dialects, then at any time the great city can be destroyed (Rev. 14:8). Unlike the Roman kingdom, which is partly divided, the ten horns of 17:13 are of the same mind. This kingdom will think and act in unison and is not divided. Their mission is to destroy the great city, Mystery Babylon and prepare the earth to succumb to Allah.

"For God has put it into their hearts to fulfill His purpose, to be of one mind, and to give their kingdom to the beast, until the words of God are fulfilled" (Rev. 17:17).

God will make these ten kings come against the harlot, the great trade city of Revelation. Chapters 2 and 7 of Daniel reveal the mystery of Leviathan's 7 heads and 10 horns, representing kings and kingdoms and are laid out in chronological order. Babylon, Persia, Greece, Rome, lion, bear, leopard and the most ruthless ten horns. We see eight kingdoms connecting to Revelation 17:11. Understand that the first four heads of Leviathan have been destroyed, Babylon through Rome. All four ancient kingdoms have been shattered and cast to the wind, leaving no trace (Dan 2:35), with the exception of ten horns which are prophesied to return and completely crush this earth. Daniel's vision of the horns shook his soul unlike the other kingdoms. Daniel 7:24 gives order to these events. Out of this prophesied revived kingdom, (Rev. 13:3), ten horns (kings) will rise and another king will rise after, for he will be different from the other kingdoms (lion bear and leopard). This king is referred to in Rev.17:10. Understand that this evil kingdom (beast) is established first then the ten horns rise from it. This is the kingdom that returns from the past and then the horns become active with the beast to which they are part of; a kingdom that was and will be (Rev. 17:12). In Daniel 7, the last kingdom, the ten horns have a descriptive nature representing an overwhelming power as they devour the whole earth, a revived kingdom that is the eighth and last kingdom of Leviathan (Rev. 17:11). Daniel's seventh chapter informs us that the ten horns are active and have risen from within their kingdom and trample the entire earth. They are the catalyst to the apocalypse. Daniel 7:11-12, are key verses to understanding that there are differences between Nebuchadnezzar's dream and Daniel's vision. The last of the four beasts, the ten horns, will be destroyed first. The other three kingdoms will have their lives spared but without dominion and this is the opposite of what took place in Nebuchadnezzar's dream as all the kingdoms were destroyed in succession, ending with Rome.

In Revelation 13:2; John saw a comprised kingdom, with a body of a leopard, feet of a bear and mouth of a lion. The mouth of a lion is Satan, which will be discussed in a later chapter. How do these kingdoms become one? Daniel interpreted two dreams which included eight kingdoms. One of the seven kingdoms will become the eighth (the ten horns), Rev. 17:11. All seven kingdoms are diverse and as for the eighth, it will not be a typical kingdom, as it does not conform to the previous kingdoms. The last king, the seventh, as referenced in Revelation 17:10, will also be different from the previous kings (Dan. 7:24); for he is Satan. When these ten horns return from their former kingdom, they will rise out of a single kingdom or this could refer to lands that Ancient Persia conquered.

Nebuchadnezzar's four kingdoms have been cast to the wind, with the exception of the ten horns that will return in the latter days and join with the beast (kingdom) that was, Persia. The old kingdoms are gone, yet one will revive only to become the most feared and dreaded kingdom that Christianity has ever seen.

Leviathan becomes aroused and leaves the bottomless pit. As this sea beast arises up out of the sea it carries with it an ancient head that is still breathing, Persia. Leviathan also brings these ten horns back to live again.

With the information we receive from the seventh chapter of Daniel, we can understand that the last kingdom (ten horns) consumes the entire earth. This would include all nations. The lion, bear and leopard will form one gigantic kingdom, a kingdom of great evil that covers the entire globe and will come against God and his saints. Daniel viewed the ten horns with a troubled heart. The horns represent the eighth beast, the eighth kingdom that comprises all kingdoms of the world into one. Especially with the help from the false prophet and the mouth of a lion, Satan. This had to be very puzzling to Daniel, not able to comprehend this, but in spirit he knew the horns were very significant! Again, it is very important to understand Daniel 7:12. The last kingdom (ten horns) is destroyed first as the other three kingdoms continue to live without dominance. So unlike Nebuchadnezzar's dream of a statue representing four kingdoms that were destroyed in succession. Daniel's vision portrayed four kingdoms with the last kingdom (ten horns) being destroyed first. The lion, bear and leopard are left without direction, without dominance for an appointed time (Dan. 7:11-12).

"Thus he said: 'The fourth beast shall be a fourth kingdom on earth, Which shall be different from all *other* kingdoms, And shall devour the whole earth, Trample it and break it in pieces. V24 The ten horns *are* ten kings *Who* shall arise from this kingdom" (Dan. 7:23-24).

"The beast that was, and is not, is himself also the eighth, and is of the seven, and is going to perdition" (Rev. 17:11).

The kingdom of evil will rise first, along with a false prophet. Out of this kingdom come the ten horns and out of the horns another king will rise, Satan. Through study this riddle gives up its mystery. The last, the eighth is from one of the seven kingdoms of Leviathan. A kingdom that ten kings once ruled, Ancient Persia, which eventually becomes the New Persian Empire.

- Cyrus founded Persia and led the Achaemenid Empire to its glory and was ruled by ten powerful kings.

- In the end times, Leviathan's horns become active with the revived beast.

- Daniel 7:20 informs us that ten kings once sat on a head (kingdom) of Leviathan.

- In Daniel 7, the last kingdom, ten kings (ten horns) are fully engaged with the beast from which they originated. They become active with the head, body and tail.

- From the time of Persian rule to the end of days, the ten horns once again become active with the beast (kingdom) from which they came. The harlot, the great city, Mystery Babylon is then destroyed.

- There was a beast (kingdom) that once existed, (Dan. 7:20) defeated and looked as though it would never rise again, yet it will miraculously return (Rev. 13:3). The entire world will worship the false teaching of this new kingdom (Rev. 17:7-17).

- Any that do not join with this revived kingdom and honor its prophet and the mouth of a lion (Satan) and does not take Satan's mark on the right hand or forehead, will be killed (Rev. 13:7, 13:15-17, 14:9-11, 20: 4-6).

- The ten horns are the catalyst to the apocalypse.
- At this time the true saints will prove their faith.
- With the destruction of the harlot, Mystery Babylon, the great tribulation begins along with judgment upon the house of the Lord. The slaughter of the saints begins (Rev. 13:7) and carries on throughout the fifth seal (Rev. 6:9-11) and beyond.

Chapter 12

Revelation 13 – Two Antichrists

"And he deceives those who dwell on the earth by those signs which he was granted to do in the sight of the beast, telling those who dwell on the earth to make an image to the beast who was wounded by the sword and lived. V15 He was granted *power* to give breath to the image of the beast, that the image of the beast should both speak and cause as many as would not worship the image of the beast to be killed. V16 He causes all, both small and great, rich and poor, free and slave, to receive a mark on their right hand or on their foreheads, V17 and that no one may buy or sell except one who has the mark or the name of the beast, or the number of his name" (Rev. 13:14-17). How do we know this is the false prophet that will make everyone on earth honor him and his revived kingdom as he gives signs and wonders to the world?

"Then the beast was captured, and with him the false prophet who worked signs in his presence, by which he deceived those who received the mark of the beast and those who worshiped his image. These two were cast alive into the lake of fire burning with brimstone" Rev. 19:20.

Comprehending Revelation's thirteenth chapter is extremely difficult and now is the time to draw upon the knowledge to which you have acquired. Let's examine these last two evil kings that will soon lead billions of souls to hell.

An antichrist is one that denies the divinity of Christ, and this affects the truth of God. The thirteenth chapter is direct, focusing on two men that are kings. Both will create and support a kingdom that will kill any that believe in biblical truth. Jesus is not only a true prophet but the Son of God. This does not refer to Allah, for he has never begotten a son.

In Revelation 13:1, John is shown a blasphemous beast rising up out of the sea with seven heads and ten crowned horns. He now focuses on a very mysterious beast, a kingdom comprised of the feet of a bear, mouth of a lion and body of a leopard. Satan the dragon, oddly and surprisingly gives up his power, throne and great authority (which has been allowed by God) to this comprised satanic kingdom. He sees an opening, his chance to destroy and eliminate the great trade city along with the Christian and Jew, and any that will not bow and worship him.

Do not confuse the lion of Daniel 7, which is a kingdom that becomes dominated by the ten horns. The mouth of a lion, Rev. 13:2, refers to Satan. The lion of Daniel 7 is the only kingdom that will lose its attribute of what it once obtained and will no longer be unique in the eyes of God. After the lion's wings are plucked this beast will become like the rest of world, under the rule of a satanic beast which all kings and kingdoms will belong.

I find it interesting that in Revelation's thirteenth chapter, John writes about the ten horns being crowned and leaves out the heads as we see them crowned in Revelation, Chapter 12. By applying Daniel's seventh chapter (the ten horns) to Revelation's Chapter 13, the pieces of the puzzle suddenly bring the entire picture into focus. Within these horns are the beast, the false prophet and Satan. John is being shown a vision of the eighth beast, the ten horns; that is the last kingdom of Leviathan, the last evil kingdom to dominate the world. This includes two kings, two Antichrists that are powerfully wicked. Let's continue on with Revelation's thirteenth chapter.

V3 "And I saw one of his heads as if it had been mortally wounded, and his deadly wound was healed. And all the world marveled and followed the beast."

One of Leviathan's seven heads (kingdoms) receives a blow, as though it was given a mortal wound. Amazingly, that kingdom survives and out of this kingdom rises the ten horns that will destroy Mystery Babylon, the great city of trade. These horns will have a part in ruling the world, but only for only a short time. An ancient kingdom will return and honor its heritage. As this beast rises, the entire world will marvel and chase after this kingdom to which Satan will give his power, throne and authority. Here we see how alluring and deceiving this beast is with the entire world bowing to it. The tempting part is not being put to death. Any that join this evil global kingdom will receive a mark on the forehead or right hand and lose their rightful inheritance in God's kingdom. The second head of Leviathan is now brought into play. A wounded head (kingdom) revives. A kingdom that was once ruled by ten kings will again flourish with the help of the false prophet. He will give life and breath to this ancient kingdom and revive it as the world becomes doomed.

V4 "So they worshiped the dragon who gave authority to the beast; and they worshiped the beast, saying, "Who *is* like the beast? Who is able to make war with him?"

All on earth will unknowingly worship Satan, the one who has given authority to this revised kingdom. "Who *is* like the beast?" Throughout the Bible there is no other blasphemous beast or kingdom that compares to the one that Satan helps create. "Who is able to make war with him?" Since this kingdom takes over the entire world no one would be able to make war with Satan's kingdom, as it is a diverse kingdom of immense power that includes a false prophet.

"V5 And he was given a mouth speaking great things and blasphemies, and he was given authority to continue for forty-two months. V6 Then he opened his mouth in blasphemy against God, to blaspheme His name, His tabernacle, and those who dwell in heaven."

Satan is represented by a mouth of a lion, which is tainted and deceiving and speaks of great things, along with blaspheming God, his tabernacle and all those who dwell in heaven. Yet, God allows this king's authority to overcome his saints of every tribe, tongues and nations of all dialects. Killing them brings honor to the false prophet. Evil begins its reign over good, but only for a short time.

It will only take forty-two months to make the world bow to their authority. All that do not have their names written in the Book of Life will follow and worship this prophet's false religion and the religion of Satan. The false prophet creates signs and deceitful wonders and

I believe he receives his power through Satan as he gives his seat, authority and power to this man. The false prophet eventually reinstates Satan's authority and power as Satan becomes the mouth of this evil revived kingdom. Satan's voice will partake in blaspheming God and will speak of great things and reign for forty-two months (three and one half years). In this short time he begins to accomplish his goal. This connects to Rev. 17:10.

"And now you know what is restraining, that he may be revealed in his own time. V7 For the mystery of lawlessness is already at work; only He who now restrains *will do so* until He is taken out of the way. V8 And then the lawless one will be revealed, whom the Lord will consume with the breath of His mouth and destroy with the brightness of His coming. V9 The coming of the *lawless one,* is according to the working of Satan, with all power, signs and lying wonders, V10 and with all unrighteous deception among those who perish, because they did not receive the love of truth, that they might be saved. V11 And for this reason God will send them strong delusion, that they should believe the lie, V12 that they all may be condemned who did not believe in the truth but had pleasure in unrighteousness" (2 Thess. 2:6-12).

V7 "It was granted to him to make war with the saints and to overcome them. And authority was given him over every tribe, tongue, and nation. V8 All who dwell on the earth will worship him, whose names have not been written in the Book of Life of the Lamb slain from the foundation of the world." (Rev. 13:7-8).

God grants Satan authority over every dialect on earth, to overcome his saints by making war with them. Every misled soul on earth will worship this evil with the exception of the true believer.

V9 "If anyone has an ear, let him hear. V10 He who leads into captivity shall go into captivity; he who kills with the sword must be killed with the sword. Here is the patience and the faith of the saints." (Rev. 13:9-10).

God gives assurance to those saints that are taken into captivity. Their captives will eventually be killed by the sword; be patient and endure. As he promised, he will avenge evil.

To this point, Satan seizes the opportunity and gives everything he has to a kingdom that begins to rise in power. In the past, this kingdom had been mighty but later defeated, wounded but not dead, only to rise again. But this time Satan's evil will pump through the veins of this beast. This last demonic empire that will encompass the earth is given a mouth like a lion; Satan himself (1 Peter 5:8). This is the kingdom that the apostle John concentrated on (Rev. 13:2), the kingdom with the mouth of a lion, feet of a bear and body of a leopard. A comprised kingdom brought on by the ten horns, the eighth and last evil kingdom on earth before the return of our Lord.

The Beast from the Earth

All Leviathan's heads (kingdoms) are of the earth yet they are from the sea and belong to this sea beast Leviathan, which figuratively rises up out of the sea and strikes (Rev. 13:1). Symbolism is constantly used throughout this metaphor. When Leviathan is aroused (Job 3:8), it rises up out of the sea to attack its next victim. The "sea" is used as a symbolic icon and has kept the mystery veiled from the time Leviathan was written. Another example is in Psalm 104:26, shrouded in mystery, as ships sail about while Leviathan plays in the sea.

Revelation 13:1–10 has been examined, revealing Satan and his kingdom. Now another king will be added, another Antichrist. Revelation 13:11–18 explains the connection of these two kings. This king is a false prophet and later gives this evil rising kingdom a voice, a mouth of a lion, Satan. He will help revive an old kingdom and empower it with the strength and cunningness of the devil, which eventually leads the world to believe in the great dragon's lie. The prophet will reinstate Satan's authority and power, as the devil proceeds to destroy and kill God's saints. By doing so, he will bring honor to the prophet. Evil begins its reign over good, but only for a short time, forty-two months. A very significant mark will be given to any that accepts the one named "Apollyon", along with the false prophet and their kingdom (beast) that deceives all on earth. Any that do not receive this mark on their right hand or forehead, which signifies allegiance to both kings and their kingdom, will begin to starve to death or be beheaded (Rev. 20:4–6).

Two Horns like a Lamb

"Then I saw another beast coming up out of the earth, and he had two horns like a lamb and spoke like a dragon." (Rev. 13:11).

Another king is now added; the false prophet. Please understand that both kings belong to the last beast, the eighth, the ten horns.

What is meant by "like a lamb?" A lamb has been used to symbolize one that is holy, true and pure or even sacrificial. Christ is portrayed as a lamb, holy, true and sacrificial. Jesus did not give a message to kill everyone that did not believe in him, unlike these last two kings. They will soon make the entire earth bow to them and honor the beast or kingdom they represent, or die. They are anything but holy or true as they have the voice of a dragon, the voice of Satan, even though they are portrayed to be horns (kings) like a lamb. One of these horns is the false prophet and permits Satan to rule over the earth with great authority and power. This beast or kingdom will be a counterfeit of truth, all directed by two kings that are out to deceive the entire world. This beast from the earth will deceive every soul through evil powers, using a false religion. The last false religion of this world will devour any that are not written in the Book of Life.

Can anyone kill this beast or kingdom to which this evil prophet and Satan honors? Who can make war with them? Without God's help man cannot defeat either king that belong to the metaphorical Leviathan.

V12. "And he exercises all the authority of the first beast in his presence, and causes the earth and those who dwell in it to worship the first beast, whose deadly wound was healed."

The false prophet exercises his authority that has also been given to the first beast, the beast that was and yet is. This kingdom will have a miraculous recovery and becomes revived with all the power of Satan and the false prophet. The prophet will give power and authority to the first beast. This kingdom was known as Ancient Persia, which is modern day Iran. This ancient kingdom will revive and produce ten kings and then after this a lesser king that will become the fiercest deity on earth, which will be Satan's finest hour. Every soul will bow; if not, off with your head, (Rev. 20:4–6).

The beast (kingdom) will rise with the false prophet showing great miracles and signs. After this, the ten horns rise and then destroy the great trade city of New York, which begets the collapse of world trade, as the fiery red horse and horseman of the apocalypse begins their ride. The vision of Revelation 13:11 is in agreement with the ten horns of Daniel 7, which eventually take over the whole earth. The kingdom of the false prophet honors the ancient kingdom that received a mortal wound. This kingdom that was wounded in Revelation 13:3 comes back to life. This is the same kingdom as in Revelation 13:14–15. A kingdom that was, is not, and will be, Rev. 17:11.

V13 "He performs great signs, so that he even makes fire come down from heaven on the earth in the sight of men. V14. And he deceives those who dwell on the earth by those signs which he was granted to do in the sight of the beast, telling those who dwell on the earth to make an image to the beast who was wounded by the sword and lived."

People on earth are instructed to make an image to the beast that was wounded by the sword, to become like the kingdom that once was powerful and then defeated, yet revives only to become a more powerful war machine on earth. The spiritual power of the false prophet ignites the world into a frenzy of devious belief, that of a false god.

V15 "He was granted *power* to give breath to the image of the beast, that the image of the beast should both speak and cause as many as would not worship the image of the beast to be killed."

The mouth of Satan guides the beast to worship the prophet's lies.

V16 "He causes all, both small and great, rich and poor, free and slave, to receive a mark on their right hand or on their foreheads,"

This mark is known as the "mark of the beast" and is associated with the beast, false prophet and Satan, but not the harlot. Examples of the mark could possibly be 666, Apollyon or the shape of the crescent moon.

V17 "and that no one may buy or sell except one who has the mark or the name or the beast, or the number of his name."

There will be no place on earth to escape Satan, the false prophet or their kingdom of evil. If you do not take his image, likeness, mark or number of his name, no one will be able to buy or sell. This would certainly mean tribulation to any refusing to bow and take the mark. It would be impossible to buy food, clothing, gas, luxury items or even simple essentials without the mark of the beast. During the winter months no one would be able to buy natural gas or other fuel unless you received the mark. In verse 16, we are told that no matter how rich, poor, free or slave, no matter how well known or well liked you are, all that reject the mark will die, unless you are worthy and only two believers have escaped death, Enoch and Elijah.

Can a survivalist escape this oncoming tribulation? Many continue to plan for such an event, believing they can sidestep this hell by stocking food, arms and ammunition or building hidden bunkers unknown to the outside world. The problem arises with verse 16.

"He causes all, both small and great, rich and poor, free and slave, to receive a mark on their right hand or on their foreheads" (Rev. 13:16).

The word "all" to receive the mark excludes those in verse 15 who have already been killed, the ones that rejected it (Rev. 20:4-6). This word also refers to the ones not written in the Book of Life.

From the death of the white horse through the fifth seal, mankind will experience the wrath of man and Satan. With God's number of martyrs being fulfilled, the killing of the saints then slows to a trickle.

"But I do not want you to be ignorant, brethren, concerning those who have fallen asleep, lest you sorrow as others who have no hope. V14 For if we believe that Jesus died and rose again, even so God will bring with Him those who sleep in Jesus. V15 For this we say to you by the word of the Lord, that we who are alive *and* remain until the coming of the Lord will by no means precede those who are asleep. V16 For the Lord Himself will descend from heaven with a shout, the voice of an archangel, and with the trumpet of God. And the dead in Christ will rise first. V17 Then we who are alive *and* remain shall be caught up together with them in the clouds to meet the Lord in the air. And thus we shall always be with the Lord" (1 Thess. 4:13–17).

After martyrdom caused by the great tribulation, with the number being fulfilled, believers that are alive will carry on until the coming of the Lord.

There is no way out! Choose the dark side and continue to live a very short life and then be sentenced to hell forever or reject Satan, the false prophet and the beast, and join the family of the true God.

Authority over the saints will be allowed by our Father (Dan. 7:25, Rev. 13:7, 20:4–6) resulting in the removal of many saints, beheaded for their belief in Jesus and the true God. The Lord's harvest will separate the true believer from the false. The entire earth, with the exception of some saints that are spared, will not only follow the beast and take its mark, they will be deceived and unknowingly worship Satan. Those who live at the time of these two kings will go through horror and if by chance they are still alive then they will face the trumpet and bowl judgments. No man on earth would want to face these additional seven curses.

- Ten horns will rise from this revived kingdom.

- The false prophet instills authority and power back to Satan and then this lesser king (Satan) rises, only to become mightier than the other ten kings. The saints will then be delivered into the hands of Satan (Rev. 13:7).

- Revelation 13:2-10 refers to Satan and the revival of Persia, to which he gives his seat, power and authority. Revelation 13:11–18 refers to the false prophet returning Satan's power and authority as the devil becomes the enforcer of the false prophet and kills any that do not bow and take the mark of this demonic dark kingdom.

- This revived kingdom is given a mouth like a mouth of a lion (1 Peter 5:8) and has the voice of Satan (Rev. 13:5–6).

- Both kings, the false prophet and Satan are portrayed as horns like a lamb, yet with the voice of a dragon, Satan (Rev. 13:11).

- All on earth will be forced to take the beast's (kingdom's) mark, or die.
- "But he who endures to the end shall be saved" (Matt. 24:13).
- The seventh and last Antichrist (Satan) kills three of the ten horns (Daniel 7:8).

Chapter 13
Clash of Two World Ideologies

At the very end, just before the return of our Lord, two agendas will become apparent. The first agenda is that the world will be offered peace through trade. The second agenda is that after the destruction of world trade, mankind will be spared for only those that receive the mark of the beast and follow Satan, his prophet and their kingdom. Two world ideologies will clash. Unlike the first world government, that represents trade with its agenda suddenly terminated, the last will succeed in its mission to conquer the entire world.

In January of 1991, anxiety took hold as I received news that the invasion of Kuwait had begun. I knew in my heart this was the beginning of our involvement in the Middle East and to me this was extremely significant. Several times President George H.W. Bush made announcements on the subject of "The New World Order." He later organized many nations to spearhead a united drive to limit the power of the Iraqi Army. In March of 2003, Iraq's President Saddam Hussein's world ended. President George W. Bush spearheaded another invasion, capturing Baghdad and defeating the Iraqi army that led to Saddam's death. Today, Iraq is anything but secure. Its leadership is not popular with many sects in the Middle East and beyond. Jesus explained that just before his coming, the world's situation would become very perplexed. This parallels today's politics. The world is changing at an ever-increasing rate along with its complexity and as it continues to spin out of control, world security is evaporating.

There are those that believe the U.S. government, which includes the World Trade Organization, is strengthening because many nations realize there is unity through wealth, which produces security. All this comes by belonging to a system that controls world trade. As the harlot fulfills prophecy of a great city ruling the world through her riches, she stands proudly waving her WTO flag, inviting all to join. The harlot not only shares in her riches, but also with economic security. She continues to smile and is economically sound, partly because many nations have abandoned their financial institutions and have moved funds into the U.S. markets. The IMF, Wall Street, Washington and other financial organizations are all sleeping in the same bed, giving this alluring woman power and control.

For decades there has been a continual fear of an evil named "Big Brother." Each year thousands of writings are produced that relate to conspiracies, describing an evil world directed by an elite group, consumed with pride, power and evil. It is portrayed as being impossible to hide from a system that is powered by industrialization and technology. Every action of every being will be recorded and everyone on earth will receive a microchip inserted under their skin. No one will be able to buy or sell unless they are part of this demonic system. Today it seems as though believers and non-believers of biblical prophecy are looking to technology that tracks every move we make. Technology that could control your life style and many assume this is the mark of the beast. There are those that believe this present industrialized world government will be led by an Antichrist, who is mentioned in the thirteenth chapter of Revelation. He will become the leader of the New World Order and is believed to be demonic or Satan himself. Some predict this man will join technology with industrialization and the distribution of trade. He will take full control of the world. Drastically and suddenly this man receives a blow to his head, shot as if dead. Shortly after this event he suddenly returns to life and the entire world will marvel and chase after him. This concept of adding today's technology and then applying it to Revelation 13:3, referring it to one of Leviathan's seven heads, and proclaiming this represents a man that took a mortal wound and survived has to be scrutinized. A kingdom takes a mortal wound, not a man. The first question that should be asked: What about the other six heads; the other six kingdoms? Be assured that no one could scripturally respond to this question unless they understood the complexity of Leviathan. Revelation 17, informs us that the heads of this beast represent mountains and mountains often represent kingdoms. One of seven kingdoms took what looked to be a mortal blow. While some wait for a dynamic industrialized world leader to rise, another event is about to take place. Revelation informs the reader that a last prophesied satanic world kingdom is mixed with a false prophet and Satan. It is of religious descent and not pointing to an economic industrialized world! Although, nobody will be able to buy or sell unless they have the mark of the beast. Those that honor the prophet also honor a system of a false religion. Revelation 13:11 informs us that there are two Antichrists and this scenario only offers one. With the chronological timing of the harlots destruction, only after this event is the mark of the beast mentioned and this mark connects to the last two powerful evil kings, two Antichrists. I'm not trying to destroy the concept of the chip, but I do not believe this is fact. There are other ways of immediately identifying the ones that belong to Satan's kingdom. One is very simple and without technology. In the first place, if any decided to remove a microchip from their body, this could easily be done. Those that join the beast could be branded or tattooed, receiving a permanent mark. This brings us to the time of Nazi Germany, marking Jews with a visible number that was tattooed in their skin. Everyone could easily identify a Jew. Under Satan's kingdom, with receiving the "mark of the beast", it would be impossible to be free of evil. This process can be offered by anyone at any time.

Over the last several decades Islam has progressed in its dominance, along with increased persecution of Christians and Jews. That is why comprehending Revelation is so important. As revealed, an ancient kingdom is in the process of dominating the world. Understand that this present industrialized world government is not the true vision of what Revelation is giving in relation to both Antichrists. The idea of two ideologies existing in the latter days gives those who study eschatology a new way of perceiving prophecy. This existing world government, without a doubt, has benefited from modern technology. So far, this world has been ruled through industrialization and technology, along with trade. Today, the majorities are ruled through the power and under the direction of a great trade city. Scripturally, Rome is not the city that controls world trade. There is a city that already exists, and unless there is a transfer of power, New York is that city that parallels Revelation as being the harlot, Mystery Babylon. After its destruction, a revived kingdom will rule this entire planet. With the collapse of the great city, the world will change overnight. In a blink of an eye this last powerful kingdom will dominate all people on earth. Satan will rise and will be empowered by this man of faith. This prophet will believe in Satan's great lie that has spread throughout the world and will eventually dominate as the world embraces this new kingdom that will destroy the earth. This last kingdom will probably not be of the industrial power that the harlot has attained, but rather a religious and political power. The whole world will chase this beast with two horns.

Chapter 14

Lion, Bear and Leopard

After Daniel's death many centuries passed and then in 96 AD, the apostle John is given a revelation. He consumed the words described in Daniel, referring to the lion, bear, leopard and ten horns. He is now given a vision of a beast that has a mouth of a lion, feet of a bear and body of a leopard (Rev. 13:2). I have not concentrated on the lion as I have with the bear, leopard or the ten horns. The reason: the lion has its wings plucked and eventually joins Satan's kingdom (Dan. 7:4). Beyond this, there is little known about this beast.

Without Daniel's seventh chapter, John's vision would not be fully understood. Kings and kingdoms are represented by a lion, bear, leopard and ten horns. Each is independent, but, as Daniel 7 explains, the ten horns along with a king will trample the earth and comprise all three beasts into one kingdom. One of these kingdoms, the lion with eagle's wings, explained in Daniel 7, previously resisted Satan's kingdom, only later to be defeated and then it will join the world as all kingdoms chase after a satanic kingdom. The first four heads of Leviathan (Daniel, Chapter 2) ruled over Israel for more than a thousand years. Daniel's vision includes the lion, bear, leopard, ten horns, a false prophet and Satan and will rule over Israel for forty-two months and co-exist in the same time period. Let's begin with the Book of Daniel, Chapter 7, and examine three of the four beasts.

Lion

In Daniel 7:4, the first beast is like a lion that has eagle's wings, and the wings are plucked. The wings probably represent swiftness. Today we would consider the United States as a nation that is comparable, since it is signified by an eagle. With its wings plucked this kingdom would not have the dominance that it once had and would be made to stand on its feet like a man and also be given a man's heart (Dan. 7:4). We are also informed that the little horn (Satan) has eyes like a man, speaking pompous words against God (Dan. 7:8). Being represented by a man must signify that it is worldly and ungodly, as this unique beast, the lion with it's wings plucked, becomes like the rest of the world, no longer special in the eyes of God. The lion could also include England since it is one of their symbols and once ruled the world. To this day it is still rather swift. Their wings are still attached, but if the opposition preys on weakness and becomes too elusive, events of unknown horror could easily weaken God fearing nations. This eventually would turn them into a beast, like the rest of the world. Spiritually, the U.S.A along with Europe, including England, has been declining for decades and one day will face God's judgment, as he will give to these nations what is due! I believe Mystery Babylon is the great trade city that sits in the United States and its destruction is very close. When it is destroyed my beloved country will collapse; her great wings will no longer carry her.

One reason we are struggling in the Middle East, is that it is hard to know who the enemy is. They are confusing us by being elusive and more confusion is added as we keep switching sides. Who's who and what's what? Think about the "mother of all harlots", as we continue to throw billions of dollars at the ones that want to cut our throats. Do any in their right mind believe that Islamic extremists can't survive unless they convert to democracy or capitalism?

Referring to the last days, it is written that any nation that comes against Israel will be destroyed. Armageddon is the prophesied event that refers to all nations coming against God's land and his chosen people and if we are still a nation, that would include us.

World opinion is changing, even within our own country. We are beginning to see cracks in the foundation of our leadership. The Bible tells us that a nation that is divided will not stand and this disturbs me. There has never been such division. Respect for authority is dissolving and this compares to an end time prophecy of the youth not respecting their elders. We are possibly at the end of a blessing that has spanned seventy years given to us by God, since we were involved with the reformation of the Jews; the State of Israel.

How could the lion lose its great wings? Possibly, climate change could contribute and factor in this beast's downfall. With increased destruction caused by more numerous and powerful hurricanes, floods, earthquakes and erratic climate shifts. Yet, I believe this country succumbs to the world through the loss of her great city. Remember, that will lead to the individual belonging to the lion (United States) to serve the false prophet and Islam.

Bear

There is an existing power that has this icon attached to it, Russia. For many years, a bear has been a figurative representation of this nation and they have loved being compared to this beast. They have been proud of the image, being powerful like a bear that is revered and respected. In further study, we find a northern kingdom, including a king which will come against Israel and this king is connected to a bear. Daniel 7:5 informs us that this beast will wage war and devour much flesh and should be compared with the second seal, the red horse with its rider given a great sword as blood will flow! The bear's feet are the foundation of this prophesied revived kingdom (Rev. 13:2-3). This beast removes peace from the earth and man will come against man, producing a tremendous amount of death.

V2 "Son of man, set your face against Gog, of the land of Magog, the prince of Rosh, Meshech, and Tubal, and prophesy against him, V3 "and say, 'Thus says the Lord God: "Behold, I *am* against you, O Gog, the prince of Rosh, Meshech, and Tubal" (Ezek. 38:2-3).

These lands are believed to connect Ukraine and Russia. Interestingly, Moscow lies directly to the North of Israel. Russia and Persia, along with many others will be drawn down to the Jewish land.

V4 "I will turn you around, put hooks into your jaws, and lead you out, with all your army, horses, and horseman, all splendidly clothed, a great company *with* bucklers and shields, all of them handling swords. V5 Persia, Ethiopia and Libya are with them, all of them *with* shield and helmet" (Ezek. 38:4-5).

The bear is also described as lying on its side and has three ribs between its teeth (Dan. 7:5). In the future an event will take place, weakening the bear's infrastructure. The answer to this mystery has yet to be revealed. In a later study, scripture will be given to support the premise that the false prophet comes out of Russia, having close ties to the Middle East. As stated before, I believe the ten horns come from the lands of Ancient Persia. Russia, being the feet of this comprised beast will support the false prophet and the last evil king, the seventh. This will give life and breath to the beast that was and yet is. The false prophet will draw all nations together and lead them to hell. With his arrival he deceives and gives hope to a world that will chase after this beast; a kingdom of a false religion. By having ties with the prophet and Satan, Russia, being the bear, would receive much admiration, praise and power. Russia would also connect to all the nations of Islam. In Ezekiel, Chapter 38, we see Gog being drawn down to the Middle East to come against the land of Israel. Russia becomes the major player, the kingdom that will help devour the world.

Always keep in mind that the ten horns will cause the destruction of world trade and usher in this last terrible kingdom to rule the world. The lion, bear, leopard, false prophet, Satan and his kingdom, along with the ten horns devouring the earth, are combined into one beast to become the most powerful force on earth and will shatter the saints and cause many to cross over to the dark side. True believers will lose their heads for honoring Jesus and the true God of heaven (Rev. 20:4-6).

In many sectors, Russia, the foundation of the last demonic kingdom, is beginning to surpass the United States in military technology and are preparing for World War 3, as Americans are more worried about money and jobs.

Many Americans are now questioning their involvement with Saudi Arabia. Recently, a U.S. Citizen, a Washington Post journalist, was killed at the Saudi consulate in Instanbul. A large cache of weapons was previously contracted to the Saudi's, yet the U.S. could continue with the sale! The Saudi's also threatened to buy arms from the Russians if there was no deal. We have climbed in bed with this kingdom and now have no way out. We have become a harlot and this is not right in the eyes of God. Eventually, Russia will have Satan's power and superior knowledge; his technology is not of this earth. He will transfer everything that he has attained and give it to the heart of the beast, to the heart of his kingdom, and then none will be able to wage war against it.

Terrorism continues to rise against freedom as Russia and Iran continue their course, antagonizing the free world. Russia's President Putin has put a dagger into the phrase "New World Order." Their goal is to destroy New York City and collapse world trade.

The false prophet connects to the bear.

Leopard

Are there any clues to the symbolism ofbeing the leopard in Revelation, Chapter 13? John is given his revelation and is shown a beast like a leopard, feet of a bear and a mouth of a lion. Again, the mouth of a lion is Satan and is not the lion in Daniel 7, which represents an independent kingdom with the wings of an eagle. Daniel 7:23 supports the premise of the ten horns engulfing the entire world. A revived empire, the New Persian Empire, will eventually be led by a false prophet coming out of Russia along with a lesser king that becomes mighty, representing Satan coming out of the Middle East, and will rise up to dominate the world. Satan could eventually be in charge of directing Russia's great army. The ten horns rise from this revived kingdom of Persia. The leopard is the largest part of the beast and its spots could signify diversity, dominating all kingdoms. The leopard's head is crowned, giving it authority. There are three other leopard heads (kingdoms) that give the crowned leopard its dominance (Dan. 7:6). At this moment it is only a guess to who the three uncrowned leopard heads are. The leopard's body is also showing its dominance by being the body, the largest part of this combined beast and controlling the world through a false religion. It will reign over every soul on earth and be supported by the feet of a bear, Russia. The whole world will marvel at this beast, ones not written in the Book of Life.

"And I saw one of his heads as if it had been mortally wounded, and his deadly wound was healed. And all the world marveled and followed the beast" (Rev. 13:3).

On the leopards back are four wings of a bird, unlike the lion's great eagle's wings. I don't believe the leopard will be as swift as the lion, but it will get the job done.

The United States of America will also follow the beast. It is prophesied that all nations will come against Israel and this would include the United States or what is left of it.

Ezekiel 38:5 describes lands of Persia, Ukraine, Russia, Germany, Ethiopia, Libya and other armies that will come against Israel. Gog with its army and other great armies will eventually meet their doom,

Ezek. 38:22; this connects to Rev.16:21.

Let's return to Revelation 13 and focus on a kingdom that receives a mortal wound, yet revives. My premise lies on historical events as the ten horns (kings) did originate in the Middle East. One day, through the will of the true God, they will be given authority to destroy the most powerful trade system in the world and with it, millions of people. As this satanic kingdom begins to rise, the world will see a man of great persuasion, creating miracles with signs and wonders. He rises first and then we see the ten horns. After this Satan then comes to power and he kills three of the horns. Revelation 13:2 is a comprised beast, having a mouth of a lion (Satan), feet of a bear (Russia) and body of a leopard, along with a false prophet. The body represents the Middle East that encapsulates the world with its religion. Russia will produce the military power directed by Satan. This all comes to be with the help of the dreaded ten horns.

- Lion – United States, England or a nation or nations that once stood for truth, believing in the one and only true God and were blessed for it. Someday the lion will be removed from God's blessings.

- Bear – Russia, feet of a bear is the foundation of Revelation 13:2.

- Leopard – The largest part of the beast representing the Middle East along with the ten horns dominating the world.

- Mouth of a lion represents Satan becoming the voice of the revived kingdom, as he continues to blaspheme God for forty-two months.

Revelation 13:2
"Now the beast which I saw was
like a leopard, his feet were
like the feet of a bear, and
his mouth like the mouth of
a lion.
The dragon gave him his power, his throne,
and great authority."

Chapter 15

Rise and Fall of Apollyon the Destroyer

In the days of Nazi Germany, Hitler did not care how he would rise in power as long as it was achieved. He killed many connected to his own party, especially the ones named "The Brown Shirts." As he gained control they began to threaten him. He quickly exterminated his opposition, which brought loyalty through fear. Even Stalin used this same formula on his own people, producing a surrounding of total compliance. I believe these horrific leaders were intertwined with the spirit of Satan.

Apollyon will use the ten horns to open a pathway, only to regain power. With this power he becomes known as "the great destroyer." In Greek, Apollyon is translated as the destroyer and is also deciphered as Satan. Through pride, evil and cunningness the entire world will be taken in and chase after his kingdom. Through a treacherous act Satan is about to make his move. Revelation, 13:2 informs us that he transfers his power to this new rising kingdom. How extensive is Satan's power? He has to possess the understanding of technology far beyond what we have today. It is highly probable for the bear, Russia, the foundation of this satanic kingdom, to receive this blessing from Satan. This technology, which possibly originated in heaven, could be used to take down the lion; to pluck its wings and make it bow down and join the world, which becomes evil.

"Let no one deceive you by any means; for *that Day will not come* unless the falling away comes first, and the man of sin is revealed, the son of perdition V4 who opposes and exalts himself above all that is called God or that is worshiped, so that he sits as God in the temple of God, showing himself that he is God" (2 Thess. 2:3–4).

"And this gospel of the kingdom will be preached in all the world as a witness to all the nations, and then the end will come. V15 "Therefore when you see the '*abomination of desolation,'* spoken of by Daniel the prophet, standing in the holy place" (whoever reads, let him understand), V16 "then let those who are in Judea flee to the mountains" (Matt. 24:14-16).

The ten horns will become instantly recognized and praised for their scheming and power after they accomplish their mission, destroying the great city along with world economics. Keep in mind that Satan likes no one above him and this includes God.

"And the ten horns that *were* on its head, and the other *horn* which came up, before which three fell, namely, that horn which had eyes and a mouth which spoke pompous words, whose appearance *was* greater than his fellows" (Dan. 7:20).

"Then the king shall do according to his own will: he shall exalt and magnify himself above every god, shall speak blasphemies against the God of gods, and shall prosper till the wrath has been accomplished; for what has been determined shall be done. V37 He shall regard neither the God of his fathers nor the desire of women, nor regard any god; for he shall exalt himself above *them* all." V38 But in their place he shall honor a god of fortresses; and a god which his fathers did not know he shall honor with gold and silver, with precious stones and pleasant things

(Dan. 11:36-38).

What I'm about to present could very easily happen! Satan is about to go on a rampage! Just before our Lord's return this man of perdition will stand in the holy city, Jerusalem, and eerily expose his dark secret. As he stands in God's temple he begins to exalt himself above God, sitting in his throne, showing himself that he is God. After this, I believe within a short period of time, he will kill three of his kingdom's ten kings, along with any that are connected to them. Many will then follow in fear, not daring to confront this powerful fiend, for he is about to attack the Jewish nation. Just think of the shock that will come to those that believe in his great lie. Even the false prophet has to realize who he has been dealing with since Satan exalts himself above the false prophet, Allah and God. As presented, the bear is the foundation of Satan's kingdom to which the ten horns belong. Could Russia, along with the false prophet be persuaded by Satan to kill any that would try to oppose and try to compromise him as seen in Daniel 7:5? The bear with three ribs clenched between its teeth and raised up on one side could represent part of its infrastructure, representing kings or kingdoms that are destroyed. This could refer to three of the ten kings that will fall to Apollyon's cunningness (Dan. 7:8) and this would gain him more power, as Hitler did. He either creates fear in the early stages of gaining his power or after when he becomes empowered by the false prophet. He has full authorization to kill any that do not bow to the prophet. His ultimate prize is the death of Christians and Jews and to sit as "the God of the universe".

I often wonder: how many times did Satan take matters into his own hands and try to eradicate the Jews? Myself, I believe he has done this many times, but up to a point! Satan is constantly roaming the earth like a hungry roaring lion, devouring anyone that he can. He has been held within limits of completing his mission. Does he wear many faces? I wouldn't doubt it. A close friend became rather persistent that I review the mystery of the five fallen kings referred to in Revelation 17:10. I finally obliged and began the study. One thing that I do know, if any are in compliance with evil, Satan will be more than happy to help them. I think he was in touch with one of the four generals that served under Alexander the Great. In this same context I would also like to examine Revelation 17:10, the five fallen kings. Who were they and what is their significance? Are these five fallen kings connected to the sixth and seventh kings? In Daniel 7:8, the "little horn" (king) becomes greater than the other ten horns (kings); this king is Satan. In the eighth chapter, another king rises out of the kingdom, of Alexander the Great. He is also known as the "little horn." Both kings are referred as a lesser or little horn (king) and become more powerful than their fellow horns (kings). Chronologically, these two kings are set in different time periods. The little horn of Daniel 7 is connected to the time of the end and comes out of the ten horns. In Chapter 8, the little horn rises out of Alexander's kingdom. In both chapters, both kings blaspheme God and exalt themselves above God and any that relate to him. Both persecute Jews and take away their sacrifices. According to Daniel 8:13-14, the daily sacrifices and transgression of desolation will last for 2300 days until the sanctuary is cleansed. This king in Daniel 8:9, seems to be a copy of Satan. Let's look at ancient history, and to me it is quite intriguing. After the death of Alexander the Great, described in Daniel, Chapter 8, his kingdom was divided among his four generals. In Daniel's vision, he was shown one particular general that eventually became a king, as did the other three generals. This king was Greek and named Antiochus Epiphanes IV. He ruled the Seleucid Empire from 175 BC – 164 BC, which covered a vast amount of Alexander's Empire and included lands that were previously Persian. He was referred to as "mad," being out of control and of a spirit of evil. If any king were to be compared to Satan, Epiphanes might top the list. In Daniel 8:8-12, a little horn rises and became "exceedingly great" toward the south and east of the Glorious Land. He was enraged with the Jews and he "cast down *some* of the host and *some* of the stars and trampled them." In the Book of Maccabees, many accounts are given to how dreadful Epiphanes was toward the revolt of the Jews. He then exalted himself above God and took away his sanctuary. Antiochus Epiphanes, the little horn, was given an army that ended the Jewish daily sacrifices. Matthew 24:15 explains that when you see the "*abomination of desolation*" spoken by Daniel, as he stands in the holy place, flee! This has not yet taken place. The horn in Daniel 8:13 is connected to the "transgression of desolation" and destroys the sanctuary, takes away the daily sacrifices, kills God's saints and tramples down the truth of God. This Greek king ruled in the same time period as Rome rose to its unmatched supremacy. Antiochus died a very unusual death and was said to die in Persia. Did Satan test his limits. Through this Greek king, he found out that deceiving was not enough. Apollyon the devil will duplicate Antiochus Epiphanes, but with his rise he will take matters into his own hands, and then destroy the world! Relating to the five fallen kings, Alexander and his four generals give the count of five kings and the last king sounds like Satan.

In Revelation 13, we find the false prophet taking the world by phenomena, showing signs and miracles and only after this (Rev. 17:10) does he raise one of slight notice, a lesser king that eventually becomes one of superior power. No man on earth will compare to the evil that he will hold. God's most beautiful cherub becomes earth's ugliest deity as he prowls the earth like a lion, spreading deceit and killing any that will not bow to his deception. Is this king geographically distant from the ten kings? I believe Satan, the little horn, rises from the Middle East, which is represented by the leopard and points likely to Iran or countries that the old Persian Empire once ruled. Turkey would be included since the seat of Satan was said to rest in that country. The city of Pergamum in Turkey has been known as "the seat of Satan." Could Satan rise from this city? No one knows for sure!

With Iran cozying up to Russia and vice versa, Islam could easily take hold of the bear and then both would become inseparable. Only after this would Russia accept a false prophet and later help raise the mightiest and most ruthless military leader in the world. He gives up his seat, power and authority and the ten horns of Leviathan will use it (Rev. 13:3-4).

"And they had a king over them the angel of the bottomless pit, whose name in Hebrew *is* Abaddon, but in Greek he has the name Apollyon" (Rev. 9:11).

"Then the fifth angel sounded: And I saw a star fallen from heaven to the earth. To him was given the key to the bottomless pit" (Rev. 9:1).

The "Angel of the Abyss" in Greek is named Apollyon and in Hebrew, Abaddon. What comes up out of the bottomless pit are locusts and pain (Revelation 9:2–12). Satan, this fallen star, has the key to the bottomless pit, hell. One thing we can count on, he will have the power to use it. There is also a dragon coming up out of the bottomless pit (Rev. 17:8). This is Leviathan to whom all the heads and horns belong. Over twenty-five centuries pass and the horns that once sat on the second head of Leviathan will again join with this powerful beast and become active and create the eighth beast, the ten horns. This kingdom will interact with Satan and his prophet. When this scarlet dragon is released, the world will be in turmoil. Apollyon, Satan, this fallen angel rises during the time of the ten horns and has the spirit of hell within him, giving power to this beast. Lucifer the devil will not only kill saints, also non-believers that resist anyone trying to force a religion upon them. After he exposes his true nature of who he really is, those that are weak will crumble at the sight of this being that is instilled with so much power of pure evil.

"Thus he said: 'The fourth beast shall be a fourth kingdom on earth, Which shall be different from all *other* kingdoms, And shall devour the whole earth, Trample it and break it in pieces. V24 The ten horns *are* ten kings *Who* shall arise from this kingdom. And another shall rise after them; He shall be different from the first *ones*, and shall subdue three kings. V25 He shall speak *pompous* words against the Most High, Shall persecute the saints of the Most High, And shall intend to change times and law. Then *the saints* shall be given into his hand For a time and times and half a time" (Dan. 7:23-25). This equals three and one half years.

"I watched then because of the sound of the pompous words which the horn was speaking; I watched till the beast was slain, and its body destroyed and given to the burning flame" (Dan.7:11).

"So they worshiped the dragon who gave authority to the beast; and they worshiped the beast, saying, "Who is like the beast? Who is able to make war with him?" V5 And he was given a mouth speaking great things and blasphemies, and he was given authority to continue for forty-two months. V6 Then he opened his mouth in blasphemy against God, to blaspheme His name, His tabernacle, and those who dwell in heaven. V7 It was granted to him to make war with the saints and to overcome them. And authority was given him over every tribe, tongue, and nation. V8 All who dwell on the earth will worship him, whose names have not been written in the Book of Life of the Lamb slain from the foundation of the world" (Rev. 13:4–8).

We have to keep our focus on what Satan, the great dragon, is trying to achieve. His goal is the complete and utter removal of the Jewish race, God's chosen ones. Through cunningness and force he betrays all. From the time Satan came to earth his campaign is to be above God. He wants to prove that evil is greater than good and eventually the world will fall into his hands. This will happen, except with a slight flaw. God will not let his remnant, the twelve tribes, consisting of 144,000, fall to this evil. They will become unreachable. Professing Christians will have their chance to prove they are wheat and not tares. God will use Satan to test every Christian's faith. Many will lose their lives but ultimately save their souls as the gate to hell is wide.

"Enter by the narrow gate; for wide *is* the gate and broad *is* the way that leads to destruction, and there are many who go in by it, V14 Because narrow *is* the gate and difficult *is* the way which leads to life, and there are few who find it " (Matt. 7:13-14).

Apollyon will do his job well, God's most beautiful cherub; an angel of awesome power. The beast (Satan's kingdom) and the false prophet will be captured and thrown into the lake of fire.

"And I saw the beast, the kings of the earth, and their armies, gathered together to make war against Him who sat on the horse and against His army" (Rev. 19:19).

"Then the beast was captured, and with him the false prophet who worked signs in his presence, by which he deceived those who received the mark of the beast and those who worshiped his image. These two were cast alive into the lake of fire burning with brimstone" (Rev. 19:20).

The beast and the false prophet will be captured and thrown into the lake of fire. Satan is also captured, but his life will be spared. After our Lord's thousand-year reign with his saints, God will have another use for this most deceiving false god.

V1 "Then I saw an angel coming down from heaven, having the key to the bottomless pit and a great chain in his hand. V2 He laid hold of the dragon, that serpent of old, who is *the* Devil and Satan, and bound him for a thousand years; V3 And he cast him into the bottomless pit, and shut him up, and set a seal on him, so that he should deceive the nations no more till the thousand years were finished. But after these things he must be released for a little while" (Rev. 20:1-3).

V7 "Now when the thousand years have expired, Satan will be released from his prison V8 and will go out to deceive the nations which are in the four corners of the earth, Gog and Magog, to gather them together to battle, whose number *is* as the sand of the sea. V9 They went up on the breadth of the earth and surrounded the camp of the saints and the beloved city. And fire came down from God out of heaven and devoured them. V10 The devil who deceived them, was cast into the lake of fire and brimstone where the beast and the false prophet *are.* And they will be tormented day and night forever and ever" (Rev. 20:7-10).

Satan, the devil, Apollyon, Abaddon, Lucifer, the great dragon, the great serpent and the little horn are of the same, and as written, he will be captured, bound and thrown into the bottomless pit for a thousand years. At the end of Christ's thousand year reign Satan will be released and will do what he does best, deceive the nations, but only for a short time. Once again, for the last time, he persuades nations to attack Jerusalem and the camp of the saints and once again the lands of Russia will become a fierce force against God. This time there is an important difference. God destroys the Russian army before it attacks the camp of the saints and the city of Jerusalem. The end is here for the dreaded dragon. The end comes as fire is sent down from heaven, consuming all armies from all nations.

It is written that Israel will stand alone; yes and no. God promised he would never take his hand from his chosen people and in their darkest hour his hand will move, destroying any and all that come against his beloved city and saints. What is written will be done.

In the end Jesus completes his thousand-year reign and at that time Satan is released as he will shake the world for one last and final time and then be thrown into the lake of fire, joining the beast and the false prophet. This will end the rule of our savior; his mission on earth will be complete (1John 3:8).

I am sure everyone has heard the claim that our former President, even our current President, or one like Russia's Putin is said to be the Antichrist, Satan. Revelation's thirteenth chapter explains why they are not candidates. Once the sixth king (false prophet) arrives then Satan will appear and expose himself. Only after does he appear and expose himself. This is of the future and do not put the cart before the horse.

The next time someone states that a certain man is Satan, inform them that he will not rise until the false prophet empowers him. Satan will give up everything to his evil kingdom, a beast that is inspired by a prophet. I would believe that the false prophet will not know who he has been dealing with. Somehow, in some way, Satan will be reinstated with authority and power and has the backing of the false prophet. Both will give power to the other and to their revived kingdom, then the world will travel through the greatest tribulation ever known to mankind.

Summary: Satan will give his power, throne and great authority to a false teacher, a false prophet that creates great signs and miracles in sight of Satan's newly formed kingdom. He realizes a new concept, a way to conquer, but not by conventional means. By transferring his power is his answer. It is the only way, his only shot to deceive mankind into believing a great deceitful lie. He knows his time is short and maybe, just maybe, he will have a chance to destroy God's chosen ones, along with the saints, dragging the entire world down to hell, which would seriously delight him. So he plays his hand and wins. Believers in God will face the wrath of these two kings, but unknowingly the ones who kill the prophets and saints will be delivered into God's wrath.

Chapter 16

Leviathan's Trilogy 666

From the time this mysterious number 666 was written, imaginations have flared as to what it represents. Why is it so mystical and so enchanting to lure one back again and again, trying to decode its true meaning? I have been in groups that have studied Revelation 13:18. It seems that letters can be generated from these numbers and therefore so can names. Numerology heads the list in trying to assist the decoding of six hundred sixty six. Do these numbers spell out names that we recognize? The list is endless. Others proclaim this number only represents Satan. Many movies have portrayed devil worshipers calling on 666 to conjure up the devil. Many believe evil beings belonging to the underworld have something to do with this mystery. I would like to make an observation relating to this number. I believe the answer has always laid in the Bible. By combining and understanding two important verses the mystery can be unraveled, only if there is comprehension of a powerful metaphor named Leviathan.

Revelation 17:10 has puzzled me, if not obsessed me to the point of losing much sleep. What is its mystery? What does this riddle mean? Who are the sixth and seventh kings and what is their significance? What you are about to acquire is what has been revealed to me. Without understanding this verse no one will ever understand Revelation 13:18. Neither verse can be understood without the other. The time has come to draw not only on your knowledge, but also your wisdom. Without understanding the chronological layout of Leviathan, it would be impossible to unravel the mystery of 666.

"Here *is* wisdom. Let him who has understanding calculate the number of the beast, for it is a number of a man: His number *is* 666" (Rev. 13:18).

"Here *is* the mind which has wisdom: The seven heads are seven mountains on which the woman sits. V10 There are also seven kings. Five have fallen, one is, *and* the other has not yet come. And when he comes, he must continue for a short time" (Rev. 17:9-10).

Revelation 17:11
"The beast that you saw was, and is not, is himself also the eighth and is of the seven, and is going to perdition."

By understanding the heads (one of eight kingdoms) that make up Leviathan, this enables us to count the number of the beast (one of eight kingdoms). The "number of a man" has to be revealed first, then the number of a beast can be unraveled. Let's review the last verse and count the number of a man.

The mystery of these seven kings have eluded everyone since Revelation was written. I am not going to concentrate on the first five kings, only the last two kings will relate to the number's mystery.

I am stating that the false prophet's number is "six" since he is a man and a sixth king. Also notice that this man's (king's) number is singular. This gives the clue of how to read this number 666. How do I come to this conclusion? We have already studied the last two kings in Revelation 13. One being a false prophet and only later does he raise up another king, a seventh king, Satan. He will reign alongside the prophet for a short time, forty-two months. This connects to Revelation 17:10.

"There are also seven kings. Five have fallen, one is, *and* the other has not yet come. And when he comes, he must continue for a short time" (Rev. 17:10).

Becoming aware of the significance of these kings and how to count their number can only come through study, then applying wisdom. By omitting the first five kings we are then left with the sixth and seventh, being the last two evil kings that control the world just before the return of our Lord. The sixth king is the false prophet and the seventh is Satan. Revelation 13:18 states "Here is wisdom. Let him who has understanding calculate (or count) the number of the beast, for it is a number of a man: His number *is* 666." Look for the number of a man, for it is the number of the beast. Revelation 13:11 informs us there are three parts to this beast from the earth with two horns; a revived kingdom that includes two kings. A beast includes kings, armies, people and any that honor that kingdom. With this verse we are given a kingdom, a false prophet and Satan. The false prophet, Rev. 13:11-18, is in context with the eighteenth verse. He is the sixth king. The sixth king (the false prophet) will raise up another king. The whole chapter of Revelation 13 refers to two horns or two kings and a beast (kingdom) to which they belong. Revelation 17:10 simply states that the sixth king is in power before the last king arrives. The seventh and last king comes up among the ten horns (Dan. 7:8) and is given life and authority by the false prophet, the sixth king. As explained in Daniel, Chapter 7, another shall rise after the ten horns and then blaspheme God and persecute his saints; welcome to the world of Satan!

Revelation 13:11 informs us that both of these horns or kings belong to the same beast, a demonic kingdom that includes two kings.

What are the odds of the number six being connected to the false prophet, the king that makes the whole world bow to him and take his mark, name of the beast or number of his name (Rev. 13:14-17)? The prophecy of this kingdom has not yet been fulfilled. The first number represents the sixth beast and the last two digits 66 are symbols for the two kings that belong to that beast. Each number is like the other, as they are all identical and of the same spirit. The beast, the false prophet and the little horn (Satan) are of the same mind. Thus 666; the last two kings belong to Satan's kingdom. The false prophet belongs to sixth beast, the bear (Russia). He also appointed the seventh king (Satan) to which I believe comes out of the lands of the Middle East. Both belong to the ten horns, the eighth beast and Satan will kill any that will not bow to his kingdom.

"And that no one may buy or sell except one who has the mark or the name of the beast, or the number of his name" (Rev. 13:17).

By acquiring the number of the beast, his name, number or likeness means you become like the beast, false prophet and Satan; welcome to their club.

This number is rather a very simple code. By comprehending the heads and horns of Leviathan, which are placed in chronological order, we can now count the number of the beast, for it is a number of a man. The number of the beast and the number of a man are the same. Revelation 17:11 informs us that there are eight beasts. There is no higher number mentioned in scripture, only a total of eight. Once again, let's list the beasts. Babylon, Persia, Greece, Rome, lion, bear, leopard and then the dreaded ten horns, the eighth beast. By counting the number of the beasts in their chronological order and then stopping on the sixth, the bear emerges. The sixth beast is a bear raised up on one side with three ribs between its teeth and has the same number as a man, the false prophet, the king with the same number as the beast, being the sixth. The bear is also the foundation or the feet of this comprised kingdom, Rev. 13:2. Satan, along with his prophet, are a counterfeit of God; the Father, Son and Holy Spirit. The number 666 represents an evil global kingdom controlled by two kings, namely a false prophet and Satan. They will do a service for God as they separate the true believer from the false.

"And I saw three unclean spirits like frogs *coming* out of the mouth of the dragon, out of the mouth of the beast, and out of the mouth of the false prophet. V14 For they are spirits of demons, performing signs, *which* go out to the kings of the earth and of the whole world, to gather them to the battle of that great day of God Almighty. V15 "Behold I am coming as a thief. Blessed *is* he who watches, and keeps his garments, lest he walk naked and they see his shame." V16 And they gathered them together to the place called in Hebrew, Armageddon" (Rev. 16:13–16).

From these verses we again see a trilogy. Three unclean spirits are coming out of the mouth of the dragon, beast and false prophet. The dragon represents Satan. The beast represents a kingdom to which Satan and the false prophet belong. The false prophet is a king that gives authority to Apollyon, Satan. I state that the false prophet comes from the bear, out of Russia, and the last king, (Satan) comes after and rules for a short time, forty-two months. He rises out of the Middle East among the ten horns. Count the number of the beast by knowing the number of a man. God saved this mystery to be known at the very end of time, just before the return of our Lord Jesus.

Revelation 13:18
"Here is wisdom. Let him who has understanding calculate the number of the beast, for it is the number of a man: His number is 666."

We are told to calculate or to count the number of the beast. The beast that was, and is not, is himself also the eighth and of the seven.

Scripture Removes the Mystery of 666

By connecting Daniel 2 and 7, Leviathan amazingly comes to light. Only then is it possible to count the number of the beast and the number of a man. There are now eight beasts (kingdoms) and seven kings to choose from.

- Leviathan rises up out of the sea having seven heads and ten horns.

- Any that obtain wisdom of prophecy will connect and reveal these verses (Revelation 13:18, 17:9-11).

- Those understanding Leviathan realize there are seven heads and ten horns, totaling eight kingdoms.

- One of Leviathan's heads (kingdoms) receives a mortal wound, yet survives, only to rule at the time of the end. This kingdom will kill God's saints and will eventually overcome and destroy the world (Rev. 13:3).

- The eighth beast (kingdom) is of the seven beasts (kingdoms) (Rev. 17:11).

- The ten horns represent the eighth beast (kingdom) (Daniel 7).

- A revived kingdom will deceive the world into believing Satan's great lie (Rev. 13:3).

- Leviathan's ten horns rise from this revived kingdom of Persia (Dan. 7:24).

- Count the number of the beast; it is also the number of a man (Rev 13:18, 17:9-10). The false prophet is the sixth king. Satan is the seventh and last king and both belong to the sixth beast.

- All the kingdoms that make up Leviathan are in chronological order (Daniel 2 and 7).

- The bear is the sixth beast (kingdom). The false prophet is the sixth king and returns Satan's authority and power to which he endows the last beast (kingdom) with his evil.

- Satan's kingdom – mouth of a lion, feet of a bear and body of a leopard. This represents the ten horns and Middle East, along with Satan, the false prophet and Russia. They will rule the world through a false religion (Rev. 13:2).

You can now appreciate the importance of understanding Leviathan. Without counting the kingdoms that makeup Leviathan, which are in chronological order, it would be utterly impossible to count the number of the beast as Revelation 13:18 asks us to do. Leviathan is the key, the missing link to understanding 666.

Chapter 17

Wrath of Man, Satan and God

Throughout centuries there has been confusion about a prophesied wrath that is to come upon mankind in the latter days, the great tribulation. Because of this, debates have flourished. Many that try to protect their scriptural premise cannot or dare not debate the subject because they actually do not understand scripture on which their foundations are based. From the beginning, God has sent his wrath upon man. He has even removed the seed of nations and used earthquakes, plagues, even fire from heaven to punish those that hated him. He also uses man to deliver his wrath, sending strong and prideful nations against his chosen ones; only to correct their fallen ways. Throughout history wars have been fought without the council of God; having nothing to do with religion. Evil, greed, lust, jealousy and pride are just part of the equation for war. This is man's wrath against man, for he will kill for his own desires.

"You are all sons of light and sons of the day. We are not of the night nor of darkness. V6 Therefore let us not sleep, as others *do*, but let us watch and be sober. V7 For those who sleep, sleep at night, and those who get drunk are drunk at night. V8 But let us who are of the day be sober, putting on the breastplate of faith and love, and *as* a helmet the hope of salvation. V9 For God did not appoint us to wrath, but to obtain salvation through the Lord Jesus Christ, V10 who died for us, that whether we wake or sleep, we should live together with Him" (1 Thess. 5: 5-10)

"So then, my beloved brethren, let every man be swift to hear, slow to speak, slow to wrath; V20 for the wrath of man does not produce the righteousness of God" (James 1:19–20).

By being told that "God did not appoint us to wrath" is the basis for some to believe Christians are not to go through any kind of wrath or tribulation. Hopefully, by now you can see the opposite side of this. We are encouraged and told to put on the full armor of God and not fail this upcoming test or any test that will cause the rejection of Jesus and the true God. Throughout the ages God's believers, even the ones closest to Jesus, have suffered horrific tortures that ultimately brought their deaths. Satan will use his power and authority throughout the great tribulation, which continues to the end of the fifth seal and connects to the thirteenth chapter of Revelation. The saints will be allowed to be put into the devil's hands and will be beheaded (Dan. 7:25, Rev. 13:7, 20:4-6). We are not appointed to anger or rage, unless those of evil agendas try to steal our soul.

A False Concept

Comprehending the seven seals and presenting them in chronological order will expose false concepts. Many scholars base their premise on misled scripture. After the white horse and its rider spread peace throughout the world, unexpectedly, in one day, in one hour, peace comes to a sudden and tragic end as a great city collapses in its own ashes. After this, the red horse and its rider will begin their ride, as the great tribulation begins to grip the world. The ten horns will play the major role of ushering in the great tribulation, by destroying the great city of New York. A great sword is given to one that sits on this fiery red beast, instilled with all the wrath and power of Satan. With the emergence of this horse, man begins to slaughter those on earth

(Rev. 6:3-4). Mankind will be delivered into a tribulation that has never been or will ever be again; this is where the mark of the beast enters. Believers and even non-believers of God will be delivered into the hands of this man of perdition. Many insist the rapture will keep them from God's wrath and that the seven seals will not affect them. However, their concept is not exactly what scripture describes. With the exception of the first seal, which represents peace, we are left with the other six which represent wrath. We understand that man, along with the power of Satan, has everything to do with the great tribulation that comes upon the world. Only after the great tribulation does God begin to reclaim the earth, which begins in the seventh seal. Only in this seal do we see his wrath. This is why the fifth seal is confusing to those that want to have faith in the removal of the true believer without tribulation. Saints will continue to be martyred until the very end of the great tribulation and will continue until the return of our Lord. The latter-day Christian will face what Christ faced as there is no way out. At the very end of days, when the whole world will hate the true God and follow Satan, the slaughter of the saints will continue to increase until the number is fulfilled.

Were the apostles and disciples of Jesus delivered from the hands of the Romans? Extreme hardships were put upon the early Christians, even the unbelievable ways they were killed as their bodies were stretched out on wooden crosses and their hands and feet were driven through with iron spikes and left to die a cruel death. Some suffered attacks from lions and dogs, tearing flesh from their bones. There were so many ways Christians have proven their faith. From the time of the early church submitting to persecution and torture, which resulted in death, they realized this was an ultimate way to prove that one is worthy of receiving an eternal crown.

Are today's Christians better off than the early Christians? Isn't it a relief that we don't have to go through tribulation like the early church; or do we? Are believers today so special as to not endure pain? Could it be that we wear better clothes or have nicer homes or comb our hair with more style to keep us from that dreaded time of the great tribulation? Currently, we are experiencing an increase in martyrdom of the faithful. Their removal is from the wrath of man and Satan and all over the world Christians are being slain for their faith. In this time of trouble comes the test of all tests. Without preparation many will not endure and will fall. Being promised by those that support the rapture of Christians before the great tribulation, throws the professing believer into a false hope and will keep many from becoming fully prepared. In this upcoming fierce time of trouble the enemy will cry out to the saint, "Where *is* their God?" (Joel 2:17).

"I will say to God my Rock, Why have You forgotten me? Why do I go mourning because of the oppression of the enemy?" V10 As with a breaking of my bones, My enemies reproach me, While they say to me all day long, "Where is your God?" (Ps. 42:9-10).

This will also happen to the latter-day believer as Satan's kingdom will ridicule and grind the saints into dust, either to break you or kill you, while saying "Where is your God?"

"We are bound to thank God always for you, brethren, as it is fitting, because your faith grows exceedingly, and the love of every one of you all abounds toward each other, V4 so that we ourselves boast of you among the churches of God for your patience and faith in all your persecutions and tribulations that you endure, V5 *which* is manifest evidence of the righteous judgment of God, that you may be counted worthy of the kingdom of God, for which you also suffer; V6 since *it* is a righteous thing with God to repay with tribulation those who trouble you, V7 and to *give* you who are troubled rest with us when the Lord Jesus is revealed from heaven with His mighty angels" (2 Thess. 1:3–7). Be worthy and endure.

The seven seals, trumpet and bowl judgments are in chronological order, with the last trumpet becoming very significant. The last seal will complete a mystery that has been rejected by the world. With the sounding of a mighty trumpet, signifying not only the return of our Lord, the mystery no longer stays a mystery. Jesus, the Son of God, through his blood, is genuinely the Lord of Lords as he was sent by his Father to destroy the works of Satan and to deliver the righteous into the family of God. Scripturally, a test or trial comes to those that have held true to the true God and no one will be removed from this earth until the seventh and last seal. This contradicts the teaching of ministries that try their best to give a picture of tranquility before we meet the Lord. From Matthew, Mark, Luke, to the seven seals, all these writings inform us that the great tribulation comes first and only after this does our Lord return! We see Christ at the end of the great tribulation, not at the beginning. In Matthew 13:24–30, God expresses for us to leave the wheat and tare together until the harvest, then he will separate the true from the false (Mark 4:26–29, Rev. 14:14–16). The fifth seal gives another picture of the harvest with more brethren being killed (Rev. 6:9–11). This scripture is also connected to Revelation 20:4. Some Christians have been beheaded for their faith, as they gave testimony of Jesus and God and did not succumb to the mark of the beast. Others were killed for rejecting the false prophet's religion. Daniel 7:25 and Rev. 13:7 relates to the killing of the believer, as they convert to the beast or die. Revelation 13 informs us that there are two evil kings that will overcome the saints and they force everyone to take the false prophets mark. By accepting this mark, one also takes the entire package; his number, name, likeness and image, and if not, death.

"Behold, I tell you a mystery: We shall not all sleep, but we shall all be changed–V52 in a moment, in the twinkling of an eye, at the last trumpet. For the trumpet will sound, and the dead will be raised incorruptible, and we shall be changed" (1 Cor. 15:51–52).

This does not happen until the seventh trumpet, the last of the trumpets and this is extremely important to understand!

"But I do not want you to be ignorant, brethren, concerning those who have fallen asleep, lest you sorrow as others who have no hope. V14 For if we believe that Jesus died and rose again, even so God will bring with Him those who sleep in Jesus. V15 For this we say to you by the word of the Lord, that we who are alive *and* remain until the coming of the Lord will by no means precede those who are asleep. V16 For the Lord Himself will descend from heaven with a shout with the voice of an archangel, and with the trumpet of God. And the dead in Christ will rise first. V17 Then we who are alive *and* remain shall be caught up together with them in the clouds to meet the Lord in the air. And thus we shall always be with the Lord" (1 Thess. 4:13–17). Who are included in this first resurrection?

"And I saw thrones, and they sat on them, and judgment was committed to them. Then I *saw* the souls of those who had been beheaded for their witness to Jesus and for the word of God, who had not worshiped the beast or his image, and had not received *his* mark on their foreheads or on their hands. And they lived and reigned with Christ for a thousand years. V5 But the rest of the dead did not live again until the thousand years were finished. This is the first resurrection. V6 Blessed and holy *is* he who has part in the first resurrection. Over such the second death has no power, but they shall be priests of God and of Christ, and shall reign with Him a thousand years" (Rev. 20:4-6).

A very important question comes from this passage. If we are not to precede in the resurrection, the ones that are dead, then when do we go up in a twinkling of an eye to meet the Lord? We are told that we cannot precede the dead in Christ, so when do they rise and when is the first resurrection so that we may follow? We now know the dead in Christ rise first, those who have paid the price for their belief and have gone through the great tribulation (Rev. 20:4–60). Later, the ones who remain and are alive are going to be caught up in the clouds with the Lord, after the first resurrection.

"But the rest of the dead did not live again until the thousand years were finished. This *is* the first resurrection" (Rev. 20:5).

This first resurrection includes the ones beheaded because of their faith and not taking the mark of the beast. These are the saints that will spend a thousand year reign with Jesus, the ones that will go through the greatest horror man has ever known. They will have the honor to be the first to reign with our Lord; this relates to Rev. 13:7-8.

"It was granted to him to make war with the saints and to overcome them. And authority was given him over every tribe, tongue, and nation. All who dwell on the earth will worship him, whose names have not been written in the Book of Life of the Lamb slain from the foundation of the world" (Rev. 13:7-8).

This would include all dialects coming under the rule of this last evil king that gives honor to the preceding king, the prophet that gave Satan's kingdom breath and life. The ones that have enough armor, (faith) will not be tempted and escape all evil offered by these last two ruling kings. They will not value their lives and are going to be beheaded because of it. These are the ones who will spend a thousand year reign with our Lord and partake of the first resurrection. The ones whose names have not been written in the Book of Life of the Lamb will fully embrace this kingdom of evil and follow Satan to his end.

"Watch therefore, and pray always that you may be counted worthy to escape all things that will come to pass, and to stand before the Son of Man" (Luke 21:36).

The only way to "escape" the great tribulation is to endure and hold to the truth. Some will live to see the return of the Lord. Others will live in an everlasting glory because of giving their souls to God. This means that you did not fail the test and have escaped all things that could have destroyed the soul. We are told to endure to the end and then you will be saved. Flee from those who will try to steal your soul, and if you are put to death, then so be it. Think about the message this verse is giving. From the time of the apostles to the believers of today, how many Christians have been martyred and not escaped the tribulation of death but have escaped having to trade their soul for a short earthly life? Enoch and Elijah have escaped, but in a different way. Because of their honoring of God, they were prematurely taken up to heaven. Their lives were spared, for the time being. Yet, it is written that all men are appointed to death and there is a possibility that these two will return to become the prophesied two witnesses that will eventually die and then resurrect.

There are some that will not taste the wrath of God and this comes through his choosing. The woman in Revelation 12 is protected and placed out in the wilderness for three and a half years to where Satan cannot get his hands on her. This could refer to the church of Philadelphia. He then becomes enraged and goes after the rest of her off-spring (Rev. 12:17, 13:7, 20:4-6). In Revelation 3:10, the true church of Philadelphia will be held from that hour of trial to which I believe is referring to the remnant of Israel, the 144,000 cited in Chapter 14 of Revelation. Beside the elect (Matt. 24:22), we are never informed that the wheat is removed or kept from tribulation while the tares are left behind. Both the wheat and tare are harvested by sharp sickles and the tares will never get another chance to redeem themselves because God destroys them with fire while the wheat is stored in the barn. Either way, according to scripture, the tare does not have a second chance, and this agrees with Matthew 25, the ten virgins. Once the door is shut it stays shut.

- God will not remove his believers before the beginning, middle or the end of the great tribulation.
- Believers will experience the wrath of man and Satan.
- Captors of the saints will cruelly ask: where is your God?
- Unless those days were shortened, no flesh would be saved. Even his elect would be lost.
- The saints will lose their battle until the Lord's return.
- After the number of martyrs is fulfilled, saints will continue to be here until the return of our Lord (1 Thess. 4:13–17).
- There will be a separating of the true believer from false, by angels reaping with sharp sickles, Revelation 14. At the time of the great tribulation half of the professing believers will be saved, Matthew 24:40-41, Chapter 25.
- The ones who have killed the prophets and saints shall go through a hell on earth and face the seven trumpets and seven bowls; God will have his revenge.

Chapter 18

Matthew 24 – The Great Tribulation

This prophesied time of trouble will not compare to anything in history or in future events. There has never been or will there be the magnitude of death that is about to shadow the earth during the great tribulation.

Sitting on the Mount of Olives, disciples asked Jesus several very important questions. Beside the destruction of the temple, two more important questions were asked pertaining to the end times or latter-days. What will be the sign of your coming and of the end of the age? Jesus responds in Matthew 24:

- V4. Be sure that you are not deceived.
- V5. Many will come in his name and deceive many.
- V6. You will hear of wars and rumors of wars. Don't be troubled; the end is not yet.
- V7. Nation will rise against nation and kingdom against kingdom. There will be famines, pestilence and earthquakes in various places.
- V8. These are the beginning of sorrows.

- V9. Then you will be delivered into tribulation and killed for the love of Jesus.
- V10. Then many will be offended and betray and hate one another.
- V11. A rise in false prophets deceiving many.
- V12. Lawlessness becomes prevalent and the love of many will grow cold.
- V13. Those who endure to the end will be saved.
- V14. The gospel of the Lord will be preached to the world, to all nations, and then the end will come.
- V15. The abomination of desolation will be seen standing in the holy place which was prophesied by Daniel. The eleventh and twelfth chapters in Daniel gives information on Satan's move against Israel and the man of perdition standing in the temple of God.
- V16. Flee to the mountains of Judea.
- V17. If on the housetop leave everything and quickly depart.
- V18. If in the field do not retrieve your clothing, run.
- V19. A hardship will come to those who are pregnant or nursing in this time of trouble.
- V20. Pray that this does not happen in the winter or on the Sabbath.
- V21. The great tribulation is about to grip the earth. A tribulation that has not been before or will be after.
- V22. If the great tribulation were not shortened none would be saved; but for the sake of the elect those days will be shortened.
- V23. Many will claim to be the true Christ, don't believe them.

- V24. False christs and prophets will rise and deceive, showing signs and miracles and if possible even the elect would be misled.
- V25. Don't be deceived because God warned you this would take place.
- V26. Don't believe any when they say the Lord is in the desert or the inner rooms.
- V27. As lightning passes from the east to the west, the return of our Lord will be as quick.
- V28. "For wherever the carcass is, there the eagles will be gathered together."
- V29. Immediately after the great tribulation the sun will darken and the moon will not shine. The stars will fall and heavenly powers will be shaken.
- V30. All the tribes on earth shall mourn and see a sign in heaven with the Son of Man coming in the clouds with great power and glory.
- V31. With the great sound of a trumpet the Lord will send his angels and gather his elect from the four winds and all places in heaven.
- V32. "Now learn this parable from the fig tree: When its branch has already become tender and puts forth leaves, you know that summer *is* near."
- V33. "So you also, when you see all these things, know that it is near—at the doors!"
- V34. "Assuredly, I say to you, this generation will by no means pass away till all these things take place."
- V35. "Heaven and earth will pass away, but My words will by no means pass away."
- V36. No one knows the day or hour, not even the angels; only

the Father knows.

- V37. As in the time of Noah, which was continually evil, so shall the end be with the coming of the Lord."

- V38. As before, there will be eating and drinking and marrying, not understanding their impending doom.

- V39. The end will come when it is not expected.

- V40. "Then two *men* will be in the field: one will be taken and the other left."

- V41. "Two *women will be* grinding at the mill: one will be taken and the other left."

- V42. "Watch therefore, for you do not know what hour your Lord is coming."

- V43. If the master of the house would have known the hour, his house would not have been broken into.

- V44. Therefore be ready, the Lord will come when you do not expect it.

- V45. "Who then is a faithful and wise servant, whom his master made ruler over his household, to give them food in due season?"

- V46. "Blessed *is* that servant whom his master, when he comes, will find so doing."

- V47. "Assuredly, I say to you that he will make him ruler over all his goods."

- V48. "But if that evil servant says in his heart, 'My master is delaying his coming,'"

- V49. "and begins to beat *his* fellow servants, and to eat and drink with the drunkards,"

- V50. "the master of that servant will come on a day when he is not looking for *him* and at an hour that he is not aware of,"

- V51. "and will cut him in two and appoint *him* his portion with the hypocrites. There shall be weeping and gnashing of teeth."

Jesus explained certain events would unfold before and after the great tribulation. Keep in mind that our Lord does not return until the very last trumpet, and this takes place after separating the wheat and tare.

There have always been earthquakes, famines, pestilence, wars and many professing that they are the Christ! I believe Jesus is informing us that there will be an escalation of these events which are the beginning of sorrows. Matthew 24:9 is pivotal. Jesus is also informing his disciples that earthquakes will not just take place in Jerusalem, as they will occur in various places. I personally believe this verse connects to the destruction of New York City. After the fall of the great city, the mark of the beast will then be offered to all on earth. After all this has taken place the time will come to all believers of Christianity to profess their faith, because they will be hated by all nations, simply because of the name of Jesus. Hatred for Christians now turns full force.

Today, Christians and non-Christians are becoming stigmatized as extremist and accused of acquiring Islamophobia. Portraying them as being ignorant, fearing all Muslims. Most Christians look at Islamic radicals as a wild beast, wanting to kill any that do not harmonize with their religious belief. On the other hand there are Christians that portray Islam as a great religion of truth, yet John informs us that Jesus is the only begotten Son of God; he is the only door to salvation. Apparently many do not understand the essence of the true God or his Son, Jesus. Allah does not have a son!

Years ago I was watching a television program viewing a coyote feeding on a carcass. Within minutes two wolves joined in. Surprisingly, all of them began to chase one another, taking turns in playing tag. As this continued the rest of the wolf pack arrived and quickly joined in. Suddenly playtime was terminated as the entire pack charged, the coyote's life ended as lunch began. Once the false prophet reinstates Satan's power and authority, this situation will more than likely mimic that of the coyote. Most Muslims are great and wonderful people, but when that day comes and the most praised religious leader since the time of Muhammad gives a command for the entire world to bow to Allah there will be no question in my mind, because of the acceptance of a great lie, their good will become the Christian's worst nightmare. Satan will quickly carry out the false prophet's bidding. At the beginning of the prophet's reign it is possible that he will endorse Christianity. This would soften many that fear him and many might just join his attractive kingdom.

I have had several skirmishes by some trying to silence my efforts. Through a popular Bible site I wrote many articles that related to eschatology. Within a few years I was contacted, informing me that a massive amount of malware had been injected into their site, which almost destroyed it. Shortly after I received another notice, as the malware was delivered through my site, then the user program that connected to eschatology was then terminated. Months later, the National Security Agency (NSA) was caught infecting over fifty thousand sites and to this day I believe I was one of their victims. Shortly after, I was removed from a commercial jet, questioned for approximately twenty minutes before resuming the flight. My website has been blacklisted and for a possible reason: I do not conform to world security because of interpreting Leviathan, along with the book of Revelation. Think about it, I give assurance to the enemy that they will become victorious over Christianity; this does trouble me but I know the interpretation of Leviathan and the harlot only points in one direction. There is a possibility that in the very near future no one will be able to interpret the harlot of Revelation, especially the way it should be addressed. Even the International Court Of Justice (World Court) will probably be an important player in condemning Christians.

Within this last decade the world has lost its ability to control major hostilities. The Middle East, throughout Africa to Europe, the Northern Hemisphere, including many other nations, we see our peace keepers failing to overcome. Every major nation has some sort of connection to warfare. Yes, there is an increase in war. Today events are much more complicated than at previous times. There are agendas from superpowers that drive the machine of war and less affluent countries are caught in their clutches and used for the desires of the proud and powerful.

In Matthew 24:10, the word "offended," (Strong's Concordance, Greek, 4624) means to entrap, trip up, stumble, entice to sin, apostasy and make to offend. The thirteenth chapter of Revelation relates to this verse, making all, the entire world to take a stand, either for the true faith and be killed or take a mark that represents the loss of your soul. Many will turn against another as hatred and evil increases. Then many false prophets will rise and the world will be deceived with the power of Satan's prophet. I would dare to say that most of these prophets will be in allegiance with the beast and follow Satan and the false prophet's teachings.

2 Thess. 2:1-5, warns us not to be troubled. When this great deceiver exposes himself there will be a great falling away. Ones that do not have enough oil, enough faith to resist the one that will be sitting in God's temple, proclaiming he is God; they will quickly fall. Since they have been forewarned, none should fall. Verse 13, promises the true believer that if any endures this greatest tribulation of all time, gripping the whole earth, he will be saved and receive a crown of eternal life. Verse 14 gives a vital clue to the approximate time of this tribulation. When all nations receive the gospel of the Lord the end begins. This agrees with Rev. 14:6-7. Verse 15 sends us back to the ninth chapter in Daniel to which God cursed the Jews for 490 years because of their transgressions. 483 years have been atoned; seven years have yet to be forgiven and has become known to some as "Daniel's Seventieth Week." We are assured this prophecy is to come. When a "Seven Year Peace Treaty" is signed between Israel and her enemy or enemies, the clock begins to tick, counting down to the middle of the treaty, forty-two months. The abomination of desolation that Daniel spoke of is about to stand in the holy place, Jerusalem (Matt. 24:15). In the middle of the treaty Israel becomes surrounded by the ones that will destroy her and the Jewish nation is prophesied to fall one last time. This could happen within the next two decades.

Satan is about to expose himself and when he does the Jews are told to flee at once, without delay. Take nothing with you and run. Those in Judea are instructed to flee to their mountains. Don't look back and pray your flight is not in winter or pregnant with child or on the Sabbath. To a point God holds back revealing when this takes place, unless from the time of signing of the treaty is during the middle of summer, then add forty-two months, it should become apparent the attack will be in the winter, which would slow travel, and if not prepared, create many hardships. At this time pregnancy would be a curse because of the sufferings that would have to be endured. If on the Sabbath, the Jews would become an easy target as they would be killed in their synagogues.

When this seventh and last king exposes himself as Satan, Apollyon the destroyer, the abomination of desolation, he knows that he has a very short time to destroy this world as his thirst increases to collect billions of souls, only to send them to hell. Evil will flow from the Gentiles until their time is fulfilled.

"And unless those days were shortened, no flesh would be saved; but for the elect's sake those days will be shortened" (Matt. 24:22).

Zechariah 14 explains that in the Day of the Lord, Jerusalem will be overcome and the city will be taken. Women will be ravished as half their people go into captivity. Many nations will descend upon her, but a remnant of Israel shall not be cut off from the city (Rev. 12: 13–14). The Mount of Olives will split in two, making it possible for the remnant to escape toward Azal. At this time the Lord begins to fight for his people. Ezekiel, Chapters 38 and 39, gives information on a prophesied attack on Israel. The Book of Joel, along with the sixth trumpet and bowl judgments, belonging to the seventh seal, are great resources to study the gathering of armies that come against the Promised Land and the Day of the Lord. God will have vengeance.

The word "elect" also refers to Israel. In Revelation 14, the 144,000 are redeemed from the earth. These are the ones who have not been defiled with women and are virgins that follow our Lord and are the first fruits to God. The true church, the church of Philadelphia, the ones that have persevered, will be held from the fiery test. The elect will not be tainted by an evil spirit. All others, especially the rest of the proclaiming Christians will have to face Satan.

A remnant, from the time of the early Jews, a portion of the chosen ones will be saved. God promised he would never remove his hand from them. If the great tribulation were to continue, even they would be lost. Other professing faithful will not be removed and will be tested.

"When they persecute you in this city, flee to another. For assuredly, I say to you, you will not have gone through the cities of Israel before the Son of Man comes" (Matt. 10:23).

"When He opened the fifth seal, I saw under the altar the souls of those who had been slain for the word of God and for the testimony which they held. V10 And they cried with a loud voice, saying, "How long, O Lord, holy and true, until You judge and avenge our blood on those who dwell on the earth?" V11 Then a white robe was given to each of them; and it was said to them that they should rest a little while longer, until both *the number of* their fellow servants and their brethren, who would be killed as they *were*, was completed" (Rev. 6:9–11).

The souls under the altar are crying out; when are you going to stop this Lord? They are crying out about the slaughter of men, their fellow servants, their brethren. This is the last of "The Great Tribulation," the time of the greatest slaughter of Christians throughout the world. They will be hunted down, thanks to the last king that reigns for forty-two months and after this butchery the slaughter will become a trickle to what it once was.

We will see the Christian, Jew and even the non-believer that does conform to the wishes of the false prophet be totally devastated by the great destroyer Satan. The apostles were not spared and the latter day church will follow the same path. The great tribulation produces souls of everlasting glory, being beheaded for their faith; a faith in the true God and in his anointed one, Jesus. Others endure to the end.

Beside the church of Philadelphia, for the saints, there is not even a hint at a possible way out when this tribulation begins, unless you are worthy. This is why the prophets and the gospel warns the believer of an upcoming, unbelievable persecution and gives answers on how to protect your soul with the full armor of God, to keep yourself from failing the test and joining the side of darkness.

Matthew 25 gives a parable of ten virgins; five wise and five foolish. The foolish virgins took no oil in their vessels with their lamps unlike the wise virgins. The bridegroom was delayed, so everyone slept until midnight. Then a cry was heard: "Behold, the bridegroom is coming; go out to meet him!" All the virgins awoke and trimmed their lamps. The foolish virgins wanted the wise virgins to give them some of their oil because their lamps were going out. The wise virgins told them, "*No*, lest there should not be enough for us and you; but go rather to those who sell, and buy for yourselves" So the foolish virgins went out to buy oil for their lamps. Meanwhile the bridegroom came, and those who were ready went in with him to the wedding, "and the door was shut" (Matt. 25:9-10). The foolish virgins said to the Lord, "Lord, Lord, open to us," but the Lord said to them, "Assuredly, I say to you, I do not know you." (Matt. 25:12).

Jesus expresses, when that day comes it will not be pleasant for those of little faith. These virgins represent Christians with half being strong in their faith. The weaker ones straddled the fence and when the Lord returns, they will not be taken. Of those working in the field, half will be accepted. Of those in the mill grinding wheat, half will be taken. As presented in Matthew 25, only half professing the name of the Lord will be accepted. These are the ones who are not compromising. The door is now closed to those who were not prepared; those not serious about the word of God. This refers to Revelation 3:15–16, referring to the lukewarm church of Laodicea.

"I know your works, that you are neither cold nor hot. I could wish you were cold or hot. V16 So then, because you are lukewarm, and neither cold nor hot, I will vomit you out of My mouth" (Rev. 3:15-16).

The issue: *the door is shut!* No matter how loud the cries, how big the tears, God's judgment is final. He gave man innumerable chances to be saved. Some will proclaim to be on the side of Christ yet acquire little armor or maybe no armor at all. A few could proclaim to be Christian, possibly for the wrong reason. Many of us want to belong to a club or some social organization, just to be part of something, to be needed, or only to interact with others. Some involve themselves for self-gain, for self-recognition or money. This is a warning to any person who claims to serve God and for any other reason than glorifying him and proclaiming Jesus who shed his blood for the remission of our sins, they will not enter his kingdom, James 1:26. Many who cast out demons in his name will not enter the kingdom of heaven, Matthew 7:21-22.

From the second through the fifth seal we see the wrath of man and Satan. In the seventh seal God takes revenge. The great tribulation has ended, now the beginning of the trumpet and bowl judgments are ready to unfold, because of the killing of God's prophets and saints. This takes place because mankind will not repent of their evil deeds. They have no sorrow and hold to the belief that they kill the saints to honor their god. Many Christians, especially in this modern era, do not want to face the reality that God would put his faithful, including their children and grandchildren, through a tribulation that cannot be compared to any other. A tribulation that is so great, so fearsome, without the armor of God, especially the helmet which represents Jesus, no one could stand against this force of evil that will not only affect the Christians and Jew, but the entire world. Many will be forced to believe in this last beast, even to embrace a false god that will only give a moment of false security.

"yet he has no root in himself, but endures only for a while. For when tribulation or persecution arises because of the word, immediately he stumbles" (Matt. 13:21).

Many will turn their face from the apostle John's warnings, not able to cope with this prophesied tribulation. Some will turn to a church of wishful thinking or even a mosque. When this troubled time comes, the lukewarm will be called to temptation, the ones with little or no armor (biblical understanding or faith) will not endure.

"Therefore, having been justified by faith, we have peace with God through our Lord Jesus Christ, V2 through whom also we have access by faith into this grace in which we stand, and rejoice in hope of the glory of God. V3 And not only *that*, but we also glory in tribulations, knowing that tribulation produces perseverance; V4 and perseverance, character; and character, hope. V5 Now hope does not disappoint, because the love of God has been poured out in our hearts by the Holy Spirit who was given to us" (Rom. 5:1–5).

"For then there will be great tribulation, such as has not been since the beginning of the world until this time, no, nor ever shall be. V22 And unless those days were shortened, no flesh would be saved; but for the elect's sake those days will be shortened," (Matt. 24:21–22) "And you will be hated by all for My name's sake. But he who endures to the end will be saved" (Matt. 10:22).

As this in-depth study progresses it becomes apparent that there will be great hatred toward Christianity, and if it were not for the intervention of God to stop the slaughter, all flesh, including Christians and his 144,000 would be lost. The next time someone paints a wonderful picture of

Christians meeting each other in the air with the Lord, *before* the great tribulation, think again. Are we so special to be spared from the great wrath of man and Satan?

Matthew 24:29-31, gives an overview of what is to come and connects it to the trumpet and bowl judgments. The great tribulation ends and the wrath of God begins. The powers of heaven will be shaken as the sun loses its light and the moon will not shine. This will ensure the believer that the Lord will return on the clouds with great power and glory and reclaim this world, which has become wickedly evil. With a great sound of a trumpet his elect will be gathered.

Parable of the Fig Tree

After the destruction of the temple in 70 AD, God continued to scatter his people to the four corners of the earth; centuries later Rome collapsed. Many of the old biblical cities became buried. Only historians can tell of how they once thrived. Apostle John wrote his last and final words of prophecy given to him by our Lord, directed to the true believer and to be understood in the latter days. A remnant of Israel survived through the blood of her people that were scattered among the nations as they held their Hebrew Torah traditions. The voice of the prophets became silent, but their words lived on. Figuratively and fortunately, Leviathan became still, returning to his bottomless pit. When the Jews were dispersed throughout the world, figuratively, Leviathan slept and became dormant. There was no more need for this dragon. Israel did not exist, so no more Leviathan. This sea beast became inactive until 1945 AD. With the formation of the new State of Israel in 1948, being short of two thousand years of dormancy, Leviathan once again becomes aroused.

"May those curse it who curse the day, Those who are ready to arouse Leviathan" (Job 3:8).

Matthew 24:32-35, since the dispersion of the Jews, the fig tree symbolically representing Israel, did not produce growth. We are informed that this land will again become alive as her dry bones come to life. Allegorically, producing leaves on her new branch and as they become young and tender, summer or a harvest is near; the reaping of the wheat and tare is about to begin (Rev. 14:15). The word "generation" can also be interpreted as "race," which could be referring to the Jewish race and they will not pass away until all these events take place. The word "generation" can also be used in this chronological time period. Let's look at the key points.

- The gospel could be given to all peoples, tongues, nations, tribes, all dialects, possibly within ten to fifteen years, then judgment comes and begins with the house of the Lord with separating the wheat from the tare.

- Today this great trade city, New York, controls more than ninety percent of international trade, thanks to the World Trade Organization. This city sits on many waters. She will be destroyed after the gospel is given to all dialects.

- From the time the Jews reestablished Israel (1948), some of that generation, the ones that are still alive, will live to experience the great tribulation, Matthew 24.

- The restoration of Israel is approaching seventy years and symbolically her branch and leaves are young and tender and harvest is near.

Revelation is giving a specific time frame; the generation of the age of Israel's reestablishment. There are debates on the life span of today's generation, which varies in geographical areas. Because the United States had a hand in the formation of the State of Israel, we have been blessed. Because of this many believe it was a seventy year blessing that has been bestowed upon this nation, which would take us to 2018. Some believe the United States will never again receive hardship and will be blessed forever, although we are informed that Armageddon represents all nations coming against Israel, which would include the United States, if we are still here.' In Matthew 24:32-34, I lean towards the translation of "generation" and not "race" relating to Israel because the events that have been foretold are now becoming reality.

Again, the important key to understand is that the gospel will be given to all peoples and tongues and then the end comes. Mystery Babylon is about to explode into a fireball, possibly within a stone's throw of publishing this book. Prophecy of the gospel given to all dialects is about to become fulfilled. Prophecy of a great city controlling world trade is here. Israel is celebrating their seventieth birthday. Yes, the parable of the fig tree has come to be, but not completely fulfilled. The great tribulation of Matthew 24 will eventually pass before the eyes of what's left of the generation of 1948.

No One Knows the Day or Hour

Matthew 36-44, informs us that only the Father knows the day and hour of his return, along with his judgment and wrath. Jesus, the angels and God's saints are excluded from this mystery. The end will be the same as the beginning and evil will consume the earth. True believers will be challenged and will be overcome by the world (Rev. 13:7). As this takes place pray that you have peace of mind and value the promised words of our Lord that he will take revenge on those who have killed his prophets and saints. Do not value the flesh, only the soul. He will redeem us to an everlasting glory.

"He who leads into captivity shall go into captivity; he who kills with the sword must be killed with the sword. Here is the patience and the faith of the saints" (Rev. 13:10).

The Faithful and the Evil

The remainder of Matthew 24 gives blessing to the servant that rules over his household and has kept belief in his master. When the Lord returns and finds that servant in favor he will be given his righteous reward. To an evil non-believing servant that makes his fellow servants follow in his footsteps, eating and drinking as in the days of Noah; a warning is given. When the master returns he shall cut that servant in half and portion him to the hypocrites, for there shall be weeping and gnashing of teeth. In the darkness of the end days, temptation will be inconceivable; bow to evil and live. Those without enough biblical knowledge will more than likely join with the beast and accept the seal of evil on their right hand or forehead, as they will be condemned for an eternity.

Chapter 19

Jesus – Center of Christianity

Without faith in Jesus, the Son of God, Christianity would be meaningless. There would be absolutely no reason for congregations to come together to worship in his name and the New Testament would not have been written. Hate is increasing toward Christianity; especially to the ones that claim Christ is the only path to eternal life. Most of the world view Christians as monopolizing salvation. Oddly, there are many professing Christians that believe there are other paths of obtaining their crown of salvation. Jesus said to them, "I am the way, the truth, and the life. No one comes to the Father except through Me" (John 14:6). With this one verse we can see why there is so much division.

If Jesus is God, where does his authority come from?

"For as the Father has life in Himself, so He has granted the Son to have life in Himself, V27 and has given Him authority to execute judgment also, because He is the Son of Man" (John 5:26–27).

Jesus receives authority from his Father. God does not have to grant authority to himself because he is the authority.

"He who sins is of the devil, for the devil has sinned from the beginning. For this purpose the Son of God was manifested, that He might destroy the works of the devil" (1 John 3:8).

After our Lord's millennial rule he will then return his authority and power to his Father and God will again become all in all. (1 Cor. 15:23–28). The Father shared his power with his Son, being manifested to give mankind a chance to redeem their souls through the blood of their Lord; therefore scripture does call Jesus, God. They became as one, sharing in his Fathers authority. After Jesus returns, he will reign for a thousand years on earth and then Satan is unleashed one last time as he will deceive the world and gather the nations to once again come against Israel and there he will inevitably be doomed. After our Lord's millennial rule he will once again confront Satan and then cast the devil into the lake of fire. Jesus will have then fulfilled the law and will relinquish the power that was instilled in him, back to God himself. Once again the Father will retain complete power, this time shared with no one. To know the Father is to know the Son. They are as one, yet Father and Son; Islam will never accept this.

A short time back there was a television program that gave the story of a Christian man who lived with a Muslim family for thirty days. Shortly after that, a Muslim cleric explained to this young believer that there was little difference between the Christian and Muslim faith. The young Christian accepted this theology. He explained that it was Allah on the cross. Before the end of his thirty-day stay he accepted the religion of Islam. Because of his lack of biblical knowledge he fell to a religion that is in deep contrast with Christianity. This is how easy it is for one to lose their crown. There are many nice and great people of no spiritual belief and others of diverse religions. The Bible explains that even a good man will not enter the gates, especially if their religion is not true. If one is of little knowledge, one can fall quickly and easily. My thoughts fall back to Revelation 14:9–11. Jesus informs us if anyone worships this beast that is to come and takes its mark on his forehead or right hand, that person will have the full strength of God's anger. He will come against the evil ones, tormenting them with fire in the presence of Jesus and the holy angels. The pain will be forever and ever, and there will be no rest.

Why don't we just drive Jesus off to the side of the page so we don't have to look at him? Why don't we join with others that do not believe in his divinity, then we might have more in common with a Muslim or non-believing Jews. If the world can cast truth to the ground then religious quarrels will ease. This could save millions, if not billions of people from wars, all caused by different theologies. Yet, Jesus came to divide and he did that very well. If Christians could just remove John 14:6, the world could begin to harmonize their beliefs.

"Jesus said to him, I am the way, the truth, and the life. No one comes to the Father except through Me."

This is very important for all Christians to understand. As Revelation's clarity increases, then the realization comes to the reader: the entire world will accept and follow a false religion, with the exception of those that are written in the Book of Life. We have to fully understand that the world will chase evil — the spirit of Satan will engage and overcome many that stand for righteousness.

I feel sad when realizing that at some point in time the entire world will be condemned to hell, with the exception of those that remain true to the end, 1 Thess. 4:13–17. These are the ones that will be left after God ends the reaping with the harvest fulfilled, the fifth seal. Revelation gives a strong message; don't give up your precious crown and join the realm of evil. The other side will be easy and attractive. Take the false prophet's mark and live an earthly but very short life, ending in misery. Without the armor of God, which includes Jesus, your helmet of salvation, none will stand through this upcoming test.

Chapter 20

Christian or Islamic – Only One True Religion

In the realm of Islamic prophecy, there are many books and internet sites that relate to the approaching end days and this can be helpful when studying the twelve Imams, prophets relating to Islam and the Day of Judgment. Both Christian and Muslim view this earthly life as a test and with the resurrection of the dead, all will be judged. According to Islam, in the last days, just before the return of our Lord Jesus, an Islamic prophet, born in the ninth century AD, hidden from the world and hiding his true nature will eventually rise and expose himself. He is known to the Islamic faith as the Mahdi, the last of twelve Imams, prophets that are chosen by Allah. He is said to resemble the prophet Mohammad and is a man of holy wisdom that will eventually rule the world between seven to nineteen years, as this rests on interpretation and not all Muslims agree. Jesus allegedly assists the Mahdi in the last great battle against evil, against the great Satan. It depends on what sect of Islam is to be considered. Not all Muslims believe in the Mahdi and this can vary between groups. Following the Quran, the Hadith (an assortment of writings) adds information to Islamic eschatology, relating to the Day of Judgment, though it is odd that the Quran makes no mention of the Mahdi. The Hadith states that a great complexity of false religions and evil will rise before the Mahdi reveals himself as he will gather nations from the Middle East and conquer the holy city Jerusalem. I do agree that the city will be taken.

There is common ground between the Christian God and Allah. Both claim to hate evil. Both claim to be holy and pure. Both are believed to have created the universe. Both claim they will redeem this world. Do we then believe in both, to be as one? According to John 14:6, "I am the way, the truth, and the life. No one comes to the Father except through Me." Although Islam acknowledges Jesus as a great prophet, they do not recognize him as the savior of mankind and the only door to paradise, especially being claimed as the Son of God. To Islam there is none other than Allah. He shares none of his power unlike Jehovah. Allah's Muhammad became recognized in the seventh century AD, and became known as the greatest prophet of Islam, teacher and messenger and is the foundation of the Quran, yet there is not a relationship as being Allah's son.

As with Christian religion, Islam also has writings that should be challenged. There has been confusion with many texts not entered in the Quran. This is no different than that of the Mormons, writing more prophecies to which the apostle John warned all to not add or take away from the words in the book of Revelation. After John's book of mysterious metaphors, written in 96AD, hundreds of years passed. In the seventh century the Quran came to be and later a collection of writings became known as the Hadith, which is embraced by many Islamic believers as holy words. Again, added prophecies that fully come against Revelation. All one can do is interpret through scripture, words that are already in the book of Revelation. All latter-day prophecy should be compared, scrutinized and laid alongside the book of Revelation. Let's look at some of the major differences between Christianity and Islam.

Islam

- Allah shares his power with no one.
- Islam acknowledges Jesus as a prophet, but not the son of Allah or God.
- After living on earth for over a thousand years the last of the twelve Imams, the Mahdi exposes himself and kills all that do not believe in the religion of Islam.

- It is claimed that Jesus will return to fight alongside the Mahdi and defeat Satan and his evil; Allah will be victorious.
- Additional writings of prophecy are said to be harmonious and accepted with the Quran.
- Any that give pleasure to Allah will receive added earthly pleasures.
- Any that do not agree with Allah are infidels and should be killed.
- Allah only loves those that are Muslim.
- Allah will be followed by Jews.
- Sex, food and pleasure is Islam's heavenly goal.
- Allah will not reign with God's son as Jesus will reign with his saints for a thousand years.
- Muhammad has not been resurrected.

The Mahdi will be Islam's primary savior before the return of Allah. Mankind will go through great suffering. His coming also launches his doctrine for the Shi'a and Sunni, yet not all Muslims believe this. He will have authority to abolish evil and destroy all enemies. It is written that even Jews will listen and follow his teaching, yet it is also written that all Jews are to be killed, Sahih Muslim. Jerusalem will become the center of Islam lead by Iman al-Mahdi. A new world government will be created in the name of Islam. He will gather nations from the north and Middle East and conquer the holy city of Jerusalem.

Christian

- There is no mention in the Bible of the return of Jesus fighting alongside the Mahdi or Muhammad.
- On the Day of the Lord, Jesus will be supported by his saints and has nothing to do with Islamic eschatology.

- Jesus is the Son of God

- Only Jesus gave the prophecy of the harlot, the great city of trade and the sequence of events before and after it is destroyed.

- Only Jesus gave us clues of how to connect the elusive metaphor, Leviathan to Revelation, revealing the missing link to comprehend this mysterious book that believers of Allah will never understand, for Jesus is the spirit of prophecy and the Son of God.

- God's elect is Israel.

- Mankind is redeemed through the blood of Christ.

- In heaven there will be no earthly pleasures, like sex or food. Our bodies will be totally changed.

- Christ has been resurrected.

The Bible references nothing of the twelve Imams, although Revelation does mention twelve kings and every one of them represent an abomination to God. Ten kings destroy the harlot and two more are included. One is the false prophet and the last, Satan. These last two evil kings will overcome the saints and Islam sheds no light on this. In the very last days true believers will follow in our Lord's same footsteps. His saints will be overcome and killed, only to receive an everlasting life of heavenly glory. Any that endure in the Christian faith will receive a new body and mind, with no need for food or sex and will not attain earthly pleasures unlike the end goal of Islam. There is also no mentioning of Mystery Babylon, the great trade city.

With the deduction of both faiths, inconsistencies rise. The last in Islamic eschatology is the Mahdi and Islam describes this prophet clearing the path for the return of Allah. He will rid the world of all evil, paving a path for the return of their supreme god. Again, the Bible gives no reference of Jesus fighting on the side of Allah, the Mahdi or Mohammad. They do have it right with the taking of Jerusalem, for one last time!

Revelation speaks explicitly of two kings that will rule the world and they will eventually be destroyed through the power of the true God. Islam talks as if there is only one Antichrist, one powerful evil king who will eventually succumb to Allah. Revelation teaches, mainly through the thirteenth chapter, that there are two kings and they will challenge the world as never before. One is a false prophet and the other is Satan. Islamic eschatology mentions nothing of this; why? They never understood the fullness of the words in Revelation and if they did this information would have been written into the Quran or the Hadith. These last two evil kings will suppress truth and kill any that do not convert to their religion. Satan will do his job well and will honor the one that revives an ancient kingdom that becomes a new kingdom of enormous power.

As the apostle John was told; beyond the words of Revelation nothing else can be added or removed and this means no other doctrines or prophecies that try to rewrite the book's true meaning. No other doctrines can be entered between its pages. The words of Revelation would then rest with interpretation. With the rise of Islam a tremendous amount of new prophecy has been added, and to a great degree, does not harmonize with Christianity.

What are we left with? Islam claims their last Imam, the Mahdi, will come and cleanse the world of evil just before the return of Allah. Christianity claims that at the very end two evil kings will rise and support a false religion that destroys the earth and kills most of God's true believers. The Antichrist (Satan) will declare his kingdom and exalt himself over God and Allah. For Satan will set himself up as thee God in God's temple (Thess. 2:3-4).

Chapter 21

Two Witnesses

"At that time Michael shall stand up, The great prince who stands *watch* over the sons of your people; And there shall be a time of trouble, Such as never was since there was a nation, *Even* to that time. And at that time your people shall be delivered, Every one who is found written in the book. V2 And many of those who sleep in the dust of the earth shall awake, Some to everlasting life, Some to shame *and* everlasting contempt. V3 Those who are wise shall shine Like the brightness of the firmament, And those who turn many to righteousness Like the stars forever and ever" (Dan. 12:1-3).

I would like to recap prophecy directed toward the Jewish race. This is about a curse that has not yet been removed. Do the prophetic scriptures of Daniel 9:24–27 warn the Jewish people of an upcoming event that will once again crush them? The destruction of the temple in 70 AD was devastating to Israel. The next destruction of the Jewish nation will come in the latter days and this happens just before the return of

Jesus. Isaiah, Chapter 66, describes the Jewish nation as choosing their own paths and not listening to God. Therefore their wise men corrupted their people and were no longer spreading truth as they set their hearts to other agendas and desires. God became tired of pleading with them as he then cursed them for seventy weeks, which represents 490 years. Israel was condemned and paid the price for four hundred and eighty three years through the power of other kingdoms, often treating them with little mercy (Dan. 9:24-27).

Daniel 12:11-12, relates to these verses and this absolutely intrigues me. What is the significance of the last forty five days? I believe the world will be in a pinnacle of turmoil and the true believer will experience a hell on earth. They are told to continue and endure.

Daniel 9:24, Gabriel explains a curse bestowed on Daniel's people, a curse that was and still is against Israel. A total of four hundred and ninety years will plague them and then the vision and prophecy would be brought to an end. Verse 26, sixty-two weeks have been forgiven or reconciled. Israel will then be left with a seven year curse.

The first seven weeks represent the restoration of the temple in Jerusalem, 454–405 BC, which equals forty-nine years. The next sixty-two sevens or sixty-two weeks takes us to the time of the Messiah (434 years). Jesus has ascended to heaven. Jerusalem is destroyed in AD 70. We now have 483 years of the curse atoned; the last seven years are still to come. Israel will eventually sign a seven year peace treaty with many and there could be many nations involved. Either the false prophet, Satan or both will be partakers in this deceiving historical treaty.

"For when they say, "Peace and safety!" then sudden destruction comes upon them, as labor pains upon a pregnant woman. And they shall not escape" (1 Thess. 5:3).

Compare this to Matthew 24:15, as this prophecy has not yet come. Verse 27 is for the latter times when a king (Apollyon the destroyer or the prophet) signs a covenant with Israel and possibly other nations. In the middle of the week (seven years) Satan breaks the covenant and takes away the Jewish religious sacrifices and offerings. The nation of Israel will be delivered into his hands (Dan. 7:25). This is where I believe the two witnesses enter the picture. Many believe they are Elijah and Enoch, as both were taken to heaven without dying; and every man is appointed to death. This is why these two are good prospects since they have not died an earthly death. When Satan attacks Jerusalem in the middle of the seven-year covenant he will reign in terror for forty-two months or three and one half years. I believe this is the time of the two witnesses. They will be dressed in sackcloth and prophesy for forty-two months (Rev. 11:1-4). Sackcloth was worn by mourners. These witnesses have to make the false prophet and Satan extremely angry, as the followers of Satan's kingdom cannot kill them.

"These are the two olive trees and the two lamp stands standing before the God of the earth. V5 And if anyone wants to harm them, fire proceeds from their mouth and devours their enemies. And if anyone wants to harm them, he must be killed in this manner. V6 These have power to shut heaven, so that no rain falls in the days of their prophecy; and they have power over waters to turn them to blood, and to strike the earth with all plagues, as often as they desire" (Rev. 11:4–6).

For forty-two months these two men will prophesy to the world and possibly repeat the words of Moses, telling the captors to let God's people go.

Satan knows he has been cut from God's favor, never again to be a part of his kingdom. He understands there is little time for him to overtake God's throne. He swiftly goes after the woman, which I believe to be the remnant of Israel. In the latter days this dragon will hunt God's elect for forty-two months but cannot get its hands on them because God will not permit it. As for the rest of the Jews, they are left to Apollyon, Satan the destroyer.

"He shall speak *pompous* words against the Most High, Shall persecute the saints of the Most High, And shall intend to change times and law. Then *the saints* shall be given into his hand For a time and times and half a time" (Dan. 7:25). This equals three and one half years or forty-two months. When the two witnesses finish their testimony they are then killed (Rev. 11:7–10).

Just imagine what the world will be going through after these two men are killed. The two witnesses have caused many deaths and hardships to those who worship the beast, not understanding their evil deception as they despise these two prophets who give truth to the world. They will do the same to the two witnesses as what has been done to Jesus. The world that follows and worships the beast will reject their message and will be ecstatic upon hearing of their deaths. Two blessed bodies will lie in the same city where our Lord was crucified, Jerusalem. Every nation, tongue and tribe will hear of the death of these two, all within three and a half days. Even today it would be difficult to reach every tribe and tongue in that short time. As communication increases, the more probable this becomes. Then a miracle takes place as both rise to their feet and ascend to heaven, (Rev.11:11–14).

I do not believe God is going to linger as he delivers a third woe (Deut. 7:10). What a shock it will be when the whole world sees these two bodies rise to their feet and ascend to heaven. At this time fear has to come to those who see them and I believe this will be an understatement! In that same hour there is an earthquake and a tenth of the city is destroyed, along with seven thousand dead. This all takes place in Jerusalem. After the great earthquake fear of the righteous God quickly enters them.

During the forty-two months of great tribulation the two witnesses have given their testimony of truth and were rejected by the world. God's wrath is now to begin as the third woe will involve the entire globe.

Chapter 22

Holding on to a Worldly Life

I believe it is in our nature to hold to what we love in this world, things we cherish; our children, grandchildren, parents, grandparents, tradition and even monetary possessions. Throughout our lives we are encouraged to further our education in order to obtain more of this world. Throughout the Holy Scriptures we are shown how man has embraced and even killed for earthly pleasures. Today, men without biblical knowledge will never understand how anyone in this world could chase after a God that loves the simple things. They cannot fathom a God that wants you to leave the pleasures of this world and seek him with all of your eternal soul. True Christians should not worship their riches that belong to this world as they are of a different mindset. To some, losing your life over a spiritual belief is lunacy, inconceivable to those that despise God. I reflect back to the time of Abraham when he was about to kill Isaac; this was a test. Did he love his son more than God? The answer was no. He was set to carry out an act of sacrifice. How many of us could do what Abraham was asked to do? How many of us could leave our pleasures and treasures to chase after a spiritual belief? Would you lay down your life for another? Would you lay down your life for the word of Jesus or God? In the face of great tribulation this is what we are told to do. We are told to leave this world behind and not hold to beloved things that could cost us our eternal crown, (Luke 9:24–26).

Aha, the life of pleasures!

"Now the ones *that* fell among thorns are those who, when they have heard, go out and are choked with cares, riches, and pleasures of life, and bring no fruit to maturity" (Luke 8:14). "But she who lives in pleasure is dead while she lives" (1 Tim 5:6).

As one can see, pleasures can draw one from the faith. Reward from God can also be one of pleasure.

"If they obey and serve *Him*, They shall spend their days in prosperity, And their years in pleasures. V12. But if they do not obey, They shall perish by the sword, And they shall die without knowledge" (Job 36:11–12).

We are not condemned by associating with pleasurable things as long as it does not affect our faith. If we replace our faith with pleasurable things, especially sinful things, we are robbing ourselves of an eternal connection to God. At the point of extreme tribulation, at the point of losing one's life for the testimony of Jesus and of God, not Allah, but the one true God; what should one do?

"And do not fear those who kill the body but cannot kill the soul. But rather fear Him who is able to destroy both soul and body in hell" (Matt. 10:28).

Throughout scripture we are told to prepare ourselves for tribulations, even to the point of death.

"Then they will deliver you up to tribulation and kill you, and you will be hated by all nations for My name's sake" (Matt. 24:9).

Take a very long and hard look at those who tell believers they are special as to escape the great tribulation.

Chapter 23

The Thrones are Set and the Court is Seated

"At that time Michael shall stand up, The great prince who stands *watch* over the sons of your people; And there shall be a time of trouble, Such as never was since there was a nation, *Even* to that time. And at that time your people shall be delivered, Every one who is found written in the book. V2 And many of those who sleep in the dust of the earth shall awake, Some to everlasting life, Some to shame *and* everlasting contempt. V3 Those who are wise shall shine Like the brightness of the firmament, And those who turn many to righteousness Like the stars forever and ever" (Dan. 12:1-3).

God made a promise, especially to the ones who persevere and lean on him in the time of extreme tribulation. These enduring believers will inherit the kingdom of heaven and are the ones to spend the first thousand years with Christ. He informs us that when the accumulation of saints being martyred reaches a certain number then his wrath will begin to avenge all that have served him and paid with their lives. Thrones will be set and the court will be seated; judgment then falls in favor of the saints. This takes place at the end of the great tribulation and then God will have his revenge. He will then shake the heavens and the inhabitants of this world.

"Jerusalem is built As a city that is compact together, V4 Where the tribes go up, The tribes of the Lord, To the Testimony of Israel, To give thanks to the name of the Lord. V5 For thrones are set there for judgment, The thrones of the house of David" (Ps. 122:3-5).

"Then the seventh angel sounded: And there were loud voices in heaven, saying, "The kingdoms of this world have become *the kingdoms* of our Lord and of His Christ, and He shall reign forever and ever!" V16 And the twenty four elders who sat before God on their thrones fell on their faces and worshiped God, V17 saying: "We give You thanks O Lord God Almighty, The One who is and who was and who is to come, Because You have taken Your great power and reigned. V18 The nations were angry, and Your wrath has come, And the time of the dead, that they should be judged, And that You should reward Your servants the prophets and the saints, And those who fear Your name, small and great, And should destroy those who destroy the earth," V19 Then the temple of God was opened in heaven, and the ark of His covenant was seen in His temple. And there were lightnings, noises, thunderings, an earthquake, and great hail" (Rev. 11:15-19).

"Have you entered the treasury of snow, Or have you seen the treasury of hail, V23 Which I have reserved for the time of trouble, For the day of battle and war?" (Job 38:22-23).

The hail that is being held in reserve refers to the seventh bowl, the very last plague that is cast upon the earth, which ends God's wrath.

"And great hail from heaven fell upon men, *each hailstone* about the weight of a talent. Men blasphemed God because of the plague of the hail, since that plague was exceedingly great" (Rev. 16:21).

"I watched till thrones were put in place, And the Ancient of Days was seated; His garment *was* white as snow, And the hair of His head *was* like pure wool. His throne *was* a fiery flame, Its wheels a burning fire; V10 a fiery stream issued And came forth from before Him. A thousand thousands ministered to Him; Ten thousand times ten thousand stood before Him. The court was seated, and the books were opened" (Dan. 7:9 –10).

"Then I saw a great white throne and Him who sat on it, from whose face the earth and heaven fled away. And there was found no place for them. V12 And I saw the dead, small and great, standing before God, and books were opened. And another book was opened, which is *the Book of Life.* And the dead were judged according to their works, by the things which were written in the books. V13 The sea gave up the dead who were in it, and Death and Hades delivered up the dead who were in them. And they were judged, each one according to his works. V14 Then Death and Hades were cast into the lake of fire. This is the second death. V15 And anyone not found written in the Book of Life was cast into the lake of fire" (Rev. 20:11-15).

"I was watching in the night visions, And behold, *One* like the Son of Man, Coming with the clouds of heaven! He came to the Ancient of Days, And they brought Him near before Him. V14 Then to Him was given dominion and glory and a kingdom, That all peoples, nations and languages should serve Him. His dominion *is* an everlasting dominion, Which shall not pass away, And His kingdom *the one* Which shall not be destroyed" (Dan. 7:13-14).

From Daniel 7:23-25, the ten horns dominate the earth and break it into pieces. In this short time Apollyon will intend to change the times and law, yet Daniel sees hope for the saints.

"I was watching; and the same horn was making war against the saints, and prevailing against them, V22 until the Ancient of Days came, and a judgment was made *in favor* of the saints of the Most High, and the time came for the saints to possess the kingdom" (Dan. 7:21-22).

"But the court shall be seated, And they shall take away his dominion, To consume and destroy *it* forever. V27 Then the kingdom and dominion, And the greatness of the kingdoms under the whole heaven Shall be given to the people, the saints of the Most High. His kingdom *is* an everlasting kingdom, And all dominions shall serve and obey Him" (Dan. 7:26 - 27).

"So Jesus said to them, "Assuredly I say to you, that in the regeneration, when the Son of Man sits on the throne of His glory, you who have followed Me will also sit on twelve thrones, judging the twelve tribes of Israel" (Matt. 19:28).

"And I saw thrones, and they sat on them, and judgment was committed to them. Then I *saw* the souls of those who have been beheaded for their witness to Jesus and for the word of God, who had not worshiped the beast or his image, and had not received *his* mark on their foreheads or on their hands. And they lived and reigned with Christ for a thousand years" (Rev. 20:4).

Twenty-Four Elders

There are twenty-four elders sitting on thrones surrounding the most significant and awesome being as he sits on his fiery throne, (Rev. 4:1-11). In this chapter John peers through an open door, a heavenly vision filled him as he saw twenty-four elders sitting on thrones surrounding our Lord God in all his magnificence. As he sits, a sea of glass that resembles crystal lay before him. All the elders then fell before him and cast their crowns before his throne, giving him glory, honor and power. Casting their crowns could represent their praise, faithfulness and allegiance to the one that not only gave them recognition; he also is the one that had created them. Revelation 4:4, 4:10, 5:8, 5:14, 11:16 and 19:4 all give reference to elders sitting on thrones.

Chapter 24

Seven Seals, Trumpets and Bowls

It is important to understand that within the seven seals extreme events take place. One of these is the destruction of the harlot of Revelation. The confusing question: In what chronological order are they to be placed? Having studied the harlot, the great trade city, to which of the seven seals does she belong? From the second seal through the seventh there is nothing but death and destruction, as peace has been removed from earth. The only seal to represent peace is the first, the white horse and its rider. There is only one metaphor that consistently connects to this icon representing peace and that is the harlot, Mystery Babylon, the great city of trade. Revelation, Chapter 18, describes how the harlot acquires her power and why she is destroyed. There is no military achievement or aggression attached to her, only trade. She represents prosperity and peace through trade, unlike the red horse that takes peace from the earth. The red horse takes peace from the white horse and its rider. From thereon there is no more peace through the remainder of the seven seals. The harlot has to be connected to the white horse. Revelation's fourteenth chapter supports this premise with the three proclaiming angels. The first angel proclaims that all peoples, nations, tribes, tongues, all dialects will receive the gospel. A second angel then proclaims Mystery Babylon, the great harlot, the great city has fallen, it is destroyed. A third angel proclaims the beginning of the apocalypse along with death of the true believer not taking the mark of the beast. The great tribulation begins with the destruction of the great city. With the entrance of the red horse and its rider; peace is replaced with war.

From the second, through the rest of the seals, professing Christians will be tested as the wrath of man and Satan will separate the true believer from the false.

The Lamb, the one called Jesus, is the only one worthy to open the scroll that is sealed, Revelation, Chapter 5. Within the scroll there are seven seals, seven trumpets and seven bowls.

Chronological Order of the Seven Seals

First Seal

White Horse and its Rider

Conquering and to conquer by spreading peace.

Second Seal

Red Horse and its Rider

Wrath of man and Satan. The great tribulation begins.

Peace is now taken from the earth with the harlot, the great city of trade being destroyed as the apocalypse begins.

"For then there will be great tribulation, such as has not been since the beginning of the world until this time, no, nor ever shall be" (Matt. 24:21).

For forty-two months man will slay man as the red, black and pale horses and their riders reap; separating the wheat from the tare (Rev. 14:14–16).

Third Seal

Black Horse and its Rider

The great tribulation continues.

Starvation, along with reaping the wheat and separating the tare.

Death of martyrs will continue.

Fourth Seal

Pale Horse

The great tribulation continues.

Death and Hades.

Death of martyrs will continue.

Fifth Seal

Killing of the saints is carried on from the Red Horse until God's number is fulfilled with the reaping of wheat and separating the tare. The great tribulation draws to an end.

"Immediately after the tribulation of those days the sun will be darkened, and the moon will not give its light; the stars will fall from heaven, and the powers of the heavens will be shaken" (Matt 24:29).

Sixth Seal

Prophesied Events

Apostle John is shown what is to take place in the seventh seal which includes the trumpet and bowl judgments. There will be a great earthquake and the sun becomes black as the moon turns red and stars will fall from heaven and every mountain and island will be moved out of its place.

Kings of the earth will hide from God.

Man will not repent of killing the prophets and saints.

Complete devastation on Earth.

Sealing of Israel, the 144,000 receive the seal of God. This is the remnant of Israel.

A great multitude of all nations, tribes, peoples and tongues, an incalculable number that come out of the great tribulation stand before the throne. These are the ones that follow the lamb.

Seventh Seal

Silence in heaven for one half hour.

God listens to the prayers of the saints.

Heavenly disturbances come to earth.

Trumpet and Bowl judgments begin.

The world will not repent.

Armageddon, the last great war is about to take place.

The Lord returns with his army and destroys all nations that come against Israel.

God destroys the beast, the false prophet and bounds Satan for a thousand years.

God destroys Leviathan, Isa. 27:1.

God reclaims the earth.

The mystery is finished. Jesus is Lord of Lords and through his blood we are saved. Death is cheated from its victory.

The first resurrection: Martyrs that have gone through the great tribulation and will reign with Christ for the first thousand years. In the closing moments of the seventh seal, the end is signified by God's complete number, 777, the finish of the seventh seal, the seventh trumpet and the seventh bowl.

In-depth study of each seal

First Seal – White Horse and its Rider

"Now I saw when the Lamb opened one of the seals; and I heard one of the four living creatures saying with a voice like thunder, "Come and see." V2 And I looked, and behold, a white horse. He who sat on it had a bow; and a crown was given to him, and he went out conquering and to conquer" (Rev. 6:1–2).

The bow could represent power, and the crown gives the white horse and its rider authority to conquer. The harlot is a great city that represents peace through trade but also deceives the world with the help of her merchants. As stated before, this city is "The Mother of Harlots and of the Abominations of Earth." Who is the one riding the white horse in the first seal? Some believe it is Christ sitting on the horse as he conquers the world. However, there is a problem with this view. When the red horse enters, peace is taken from the earth. When our Lord returns, he comes back to reclaim the earth, and when he does there will be a loud shout, literally heard around the world. Then we know the mystery is finished, and the world, at least what is left of it, will come to Zion to worship the true God. There are no more seals to be opened after his return. Therefore, the one sitting on the white horse cannot represent Christ. The white horse has to represent the harlot, the great city spreading peace through trade. She conquers nations through her seduction of riches and peace as she shares her golden cup. It is written that this white horse is "conquering and to conquer." These words could be telling us that at the time of the harlot's destruction she is still conquering. Although scripture informs us that this city will reign over all kings of the earth, all nations will drink and become drunk through her wine of wrath and all nations will eventually fornicate with her. Many times nations crumble and are rebuilt. The harlot is always busy convincing any nation to come under her economic umbrella; to become economically secure, plus rich. She is also in an ongoing economic war as she conquers and goes forth conquering.

Second Seal – Red Horse and Its Rider

"When He opened the second seal, I heard the second living creature saying, "Come and see." Another horse, fiery red, went out. And it was granted to the one who sat on it to take peace from the earth, and that *people* should kill one another; and there was given to him a great sword" (Rev. 6:3–4).

The red horse represents war. This rider takes peace from the white horse. We are informed by Revelation's fourteenth chapter that the second of three angels proclaims that Babylon the great city or harlot is then destroyed. It is very important to understand that the great city is destroyed after the gospel of our Lord has been given to all dialects, to all peoples and this possibly could be achieved within a decade or two of publishing this book. The rider of the red horse is given a great sword and a great loss of life will follow. The great tribulation begins with a vengeance and this connects to Revelation 13:2, Russia, being the support of this evil empire, will immediately be engaged in war and will be backed by the Middle East.

Third Seal – Black Horse and Its Rider

"When He opened the third seal, I heard the third living creature say, "Come and see." So I looked, and behold, a black horse, and he who sat on it had a pair of scales in his hand. V6 And I heard a voice in the midst of the four living creatures saying, "A quart of wheat for a denarius, and three quarts of barley for a denarius; and do not harm the oil and the wine" (Rev. 6:5-6).

This figurative beast represents the scarcity of food that was created by war and its rider also carries a pair of scales in his hand. The scales could represent how far man is allowed to go before God ends the great tribulation or it could represent how much hunger, pestilence and calamity will be inflicted upon mankind as in Job 6:2. Famine consumes the world, yet a command is given not to harm the oil or the wine.

This next verse is not in the third seal and connects a very end event, although it does give a possible clue to what "wine" represents. (Rev 14:19-20).

"So the angel thrust his sickle into the earth and gathered the vine of the earth, and threw *it* into the great winepress of the wrath of God. V20 And the winepress was trampled outside the city, and blood came out of the winepress, up to the horses bridles, for one thousand six hundred furlongs" (Rev. 14:19-20).

What does this refer to, "Do not harm the oil and the wine?" At this period of time could "oil" represent the rich and the powerful that support Satan's kingdom? Could the "wine" refer to the ones that are doing the reaping with sharp sickles, the dark angels of Satan and connect to the grapes in Revelation, Chapter 14?

Fourth Seal – Pale Horse and Its Rider

"When He opened the fourth seal, I heard the voice of the fourth living creature saying, "Come and see." V8 So I looked, and behold, a pale horse. And the name of him who sat on it was Death, and Hades followed with him. And power was given to them over a fourth of the earth, to kill with sword, with hunger, with death, and by the beasts of the earth" (Rev. 6:7-8).

The pale horse and its rider represent death as hell follows. Over a quarter of the earth will be given power to kill with the sword. "Beasts" represent kingdoms as they destroy mankind. Hunger prevails as hell swallows up unsaved souls.

Fifth Seal – Death of Martyrs Continue

"When He opened the fifth seal, I saw under the altar the souls of those who had been slain for the word of God and for the testimony which they held. V10 And they cried with a loud voice, saying, "How long, O Lord, holy and true, until You judge and avenge our blood on those who dwell on the earth?" V11 Then a white robe was given to each of them; and it was said to them that they should rest a little while longer, until both *the number of* their fellow servants and their brethren, who would be killed as they *were*, was completed" (Rev. 6:9–11).

These are souls of those who have been slain for the testimony of Jesus and God (Rev. 20:4-6). They are under the altar crying out; when are you going to end this? He responds and tells them not until more of their fellow servants and brethren have been killed and the number fulfilled. When this has been completed the great tribulation of the saints lessens. This is the beginning of the end of the Gentile rule.

Sixth Seal – What Is To Come

John is now shown a vision of unmatched horror that is about to be unleashed on the entire world; as it is a precursor concerning the godly and the ungodly. Men will hide in caves and in the rocks of mountains in dread of God's wrath. Fear will enter everyone, especially the ones who have killed God's prophets and saints. The Day of the Lord is about to devastate the entire globe. Realize that John's vision in the sixth seal does not take place until the seventh seal is broken. He is given a panoramic view of events that will take place; possibly within the sixth seal. Just short of two thousand years will pass and then his vision will become reality.

"I looked when He opened the sixth seal, and behold, there was a great earthquake; and the sun became black as sackcloth of hair, and the moon became like blood. V13 And the stars of heaven fell to the earth, as a fig tree drops its late figs when it is shaken by a mighty wind. V14 Then the sky receded as a scroll when it is rolled up, and every mountain and island was moved out of its place. V 15 And the kings of the earth, the great men, the rich men, the commanders, the mighty men, every slave and every free man, hid themselves in the caves and in the rocks of the mountains, V16 and said to the mountains and rocks, "Fall on us and hide us from the face of Him who sits on the throne and from the wrath of the Lamb! V17 For the great day of His wrath has come, and who is able to stand?" (Rev. 6:12-17).

The sixth seal opens with a great earthquake. The sun becomes black and the moon becomes like blood. "Blood" probably represents the color red. Could there be a disturbance in the earth's atmosphere. Worldly events, like wars, volcanoes, or even asteroids hitting the earth could cause the lack of sunlight, causing the moon to turn the color red or something happens to the sun as it casts an ominous red glow upon the moon? The sky recedes as a scroll and every mountain and island is moved out of place. Could this be a large meteorite striking the earth?

Revelation, Chapter 7, which is part of the sixth seal, begins with four angels that are instructed by another angel to hold back the four winds on earth until the 144,000 (the remnant of Israel) have been sealed on the forehead. These are the ones redeemed by the blood of Jesus; these are the elect of God. This is a remnant of Israel that will follow the lamb described in the fourteenth chapter; the twelve tribes of Israel. The seal of God's elect takes place after the great tribulation, just before God's wrath. John is then shown a great multitude of all nations, tribes, peoples and tongues, a number that no one could count. They were dressed in white robes with palm branches in their hands as they praised God and the Lamb. These are the ones that have gone through the great tribulation and connect to Revelation 20:4-6. These are the true believers that have been beheaded for their testimony of Jesus and God, not Allah, and have not taken the mark of the beast. They have washed their robes and made them white through the blood of the Lamb. These are the ones that will share in the first resurrection (Rev. 20:4-6), and the thousand-year reign with Christ, along with the remnant of Israel, the 144,000.

John has been given a vision of man killing man, all endowed with the spirit of Satan. God now prepares to destroy the wicked. Events of the seventh seal are about to unfold. God's judgment is about to take place. He is about to unleash his fury. Three woes come to mankind, and as prophesied, there will be no grace.

Seventh Seal – Silence in Heaven

The Day of the Lord is about to begin. This seal opens with silence in heaven for about a half hour. Seven angels stand before God as another angel presents a golden censer and stands at a golden altar. He is given much incense and offers it to God as smoke begins to rise along with prayers of saints that have been killed. This connects to Rev. 20:4-6 and the fifth seal. He listens and then decides. With judgment falling in favor of the saints it is time to begin his revenge. The angel then filled the censer with fire from the altar and threw it to earth, producing noises, thundering, lightning and an earthquake. Seven angels then prepared to blow their trumpets, which will signify the beginning of a terrific hell that will consume mankind. The 144,000 have now been sealed and hidden to where Satan cannot kill them, referring to Revelation 12:6. As fear fills the earth there is no repentance by those who have killed the prophets and saints. Seven angels stand, each holding a trumpet and also in the sixteenth chapter there are seven bowls and are placed in chronological order. When each bowl is poured, God's wrath is increased, yet the world will not repent and change their direction of evil. The first angel raises his trumpet as a deafening sound denotes an action, filling all on earth with fear as many discover there is no place to hide. The trumpet and bowl judgments signify God's wrath and are placed in chronological order.

First Trumpet Blown

"The first angel sounded: And hail and fire followed, mingled with blood, and they were thrown to the earth. And a third of the trees were burned up, and all green grass was burned up" (Rev. 8:7).

Hail and fire are mixed with blood. Could blood represent the killing of mankind? Clouds are referenced within these last events and this could be why hail is connected to this upcoming curse. It also would not be unusual for small meteorites to precede a large asteroid as space rocks enter our atmosphere and if numerous and large enough, fires could be ignited throughout the world. With these hot glowing rocks hitting earth this could be the reason that a third of the trees burn along with all green grasses of the entire planet. No one can claim this event with certainty.

First Bowl Poured

"So the first went and poured out his bowl upon the earth, and a foul and loathsome sore came upon the men who had the mark of the beast and those who worshiped his image" (Rev.16:2).

A false religion begins to reel in agony as a question of doubt begins to rise. Those taking the mark of the beast suffer because of a vulgar sore. Disbelief has to come to those that follow the beast and possibly begin to question their god. "Didn't we do all of what Allah has asked? Why are we being tormented?" They still will not repent so God completes the first curse by pouring out more tribulation on earth, revenging those who have killed his prophets and saints. Paralleling these judgments are the two witnesses (Revelation's eleventh chapter) proclaiming truth to the world, which will continue for forty-two months.

Second Trumpet Blown

"Then the second angel sounded: And *something* like a great mountain burning with fire was thrown into the sea, and a third of the sea became blood. V9 And a third of the living creatures in the sea died, and a third of the ships were destroyed" (Rev. 8:8–9).

Compare Revelation 8:8–11, the second and third trumpet judgments to Revelation 16:3–7, the second and third bowl judgments. In Revelation 8:8, John describes "*something* like a great mountain burning with fire" striking the sea. When this mountain strikes, one third of the sea creatures die and one third of the ships are destroyed. The word "blood" seems to connect to the killing of sea creatures. This sounds like a large asteroid striking earth.

Second Bowl Poured

"Then the second angel poured out his bowl on the sea, and it became blood as of a dead *man*; and every living creature in the sea died" (Rev. 16:3).

First, a third of the sea creatures die and later they all die because of the second bowl being poured. The sea will cease from supplying the world with food. Again, because man will not repent, the plague is increased.

Third Trumpet Blown

"Then the third angel sounded: And a great star fell from heaven, burning like a torch, and it fell on a third of the rivers and on the springs of water. V11 The name of the star is Wormwood. A third of the waters became wormwood, and many men died from the water, because it was made bitter" (Rev. 8:10–11).

In Revelation 8:10, John sees another object falling, this time striking land. When earth is crushed by this second object, it is reasonable that billions of tons of terrain would be cast into the atmosphere. This would shut out light from the sky and produce a shock wave that would spread around the globe, leaving many cities completely destroyed as clouds rise miles high to bring darkness and death, along with great hail. Man will flee to mountains and caves and try to hide from the face of him who sits upon the throne, for the great day of his wrath has come; who is able to stand? The burning mountain in the second trumpet appears to strike the ocean. Here I believe the result of the second and third trumpet judgments can be interpreted literally, describing asteroids striking earth, with both causing great calamity.

Third Bowl Poured

"Then the third angel poured out his bowl on the rivers and springs of water, and they became blood. V5 And I heard the angel of the waters saying: "You are righteous, O Lord, The One who is and who was and who is to be, Because You have judged these things. V6 For they have shed the blood of saints and prophets, And You have given them blood to drink, For it is their just due." V7 And I heard another from the altar saying, "Even so, Lord God Almighty, true and righteous *are* Your judgments"' (Rev. 16:4–7).

God said he would avenge the blood of his prophets and saints. The time has come to repay man. Look back to the time of Moses when the seven plagues were cast upon Egypt and one of the plagues was turning water into blood, making it undrinkable. This curse sounds like it will return, but this time the whole physical world will be involved!

Fourth Trumpet Blown

"Then the fourth angel sounded: And a third of the sun was struck, a third of the moon, and a third of the stars, so that a third of them were darkened. A third of the day did not shine, and likewise the night. V13 And I looked, and I heard an angel flying through the midst of heaven, saying with a loud voice, "Woe, woe, woe to the inhabitants of the earth, because of the remaining blasts of the trumpet of the three angels who are about to sound!" (Rev. 8:12–13).

Darkness could be attributed to both asteroids striking earth. With the planet wrapped in clouds, with minimal sunlight, famine, pestilence and death would overwhelm the world.

Fourth Bowl Poured

"Then the fourth angel poured out his bowl on the sun, and power was given to him to scorch men with fire. V9 And men were scorched with great heat, and they blasphemed the name of God who has power over these plagues; and they did not repent and give Him glory" (Rev. 16:8–9). Isaiah 51:6 explains the earth will wear out like an old garment. This curse could hasten the process.

Mankind continues to be tormented as the world travels through excessive climate change; from bitterly cold to the extreme intense heat. Even though mankind continues on, they still will not bend a knee and repent.

What is going on with the sun? Today, scientists are becoming exceedingly nervous. For many decades our planet's magnetism has declined, so much that it is now attributed to the earth's magnetic poles moving from of their previous norm and at an incredible increasing rate. The North and South poles are traveling towards one another, which scientist have predicted for many years and believe there will be a reversal of our planet's magnetic poles. With the sudden decline in the earth's magnetic shield we are vulnerable to the power of the sun. This shield has been weakening, but in the last two decades this rate of failure has increased. If the sun becomes too intense, the earth will fry as its protective shield fails, projecting a tremendous amount of energy and just about anything that runs on electricity would succumb to powerful electromagnetic pulses induced by the sun. There would also be changes in geology, along with volcanic activity. Magnitude of earthquakes would increase, more likely than at any time of man's existence. Hurricanes of enormous destruction, beyond what we have experienced, will roam the seas and destroy anything they touch. Revelation 16:12, the great river Euphrates could easily connect to the sun scorching the earth. It is prophesied that it will dry up to prepare the armies coming from the East. I believe this relates to why horses are used in the last great battle against Israel. Anything that runs on electricity might not operate.

Fifth Trumpet Blown

"Then the fifth angel sounded: And I saw a star fallen from heaven to the earth. To him was given the key to the bottomless pit. V2. And he opened the bottomless pit, and smoke arose out of the pit like the smoke of a great furnace. So the sun and the air were darkened because of the smoke of the pit. V3. Then out of the smoke locusts came upon the earth. And to them was given power, as the scorpions of the earth have power. V4. They were commanded not to harm the grass of the earth, or any green thing, or any tree, but only those men who do not have the seal of God on their foreheads. V5. And they were not given *authority* to kill them, but to torment them *for* five months. Their torment *was* like the torment of a scorpion when it strikes a man. V6. In those days men will seek death and will not find it; they will desire to die, and death will flee from them. V7. The shape of the locusts was like horses prepared for battle. On their heads were crowns of something like gold, and their faces *were* like the faces of men. V8. They had hair like women's hair, and their teeth were like lions' *teeth*. V9. And they had breastplates like breastplates of iron, and the sound of their wings *was* like the sound of chariots with many horses running into battle. V10. They had tails like scorpions, and there were stings in their tails. Their power *was* to hurt men five months. V11. And they had as king over them the angel of the bottomless pit, whose name in Hebrew is Abaddon, but in Greek he has the name Apollyon. V12 One woe is past. Behold, still two more woes are coming after these things" (Rev. 9:1–12).

The ones that do not have the seal of God on their foreheads will eventually be cast into hell; they will be stung by these locusts. The irony: these are the ones who have helped Satan to do his job and killed the believers of the true God. They have followed the great dragon to the gates of hell and probably without knowing it, they will endure a painful hell forever!

The locusts are told not to kill, only to sting and torment men that have followed the beast. The agony lasts for five months and mankind will wish they could die, but will not. These locusts are like horses prepared to go into battle and on their heads are crowns of, something like gold. Their faces are like faces of men. They have hair like women and teeth like lions and breastplates like iron with wings that have the sound of racing chariots and horses going into battle. They have tails like scorpions with stingers and the power to hurt men for five months.

"And they had as king over them the angel of the bottomless pit, whose name in Hebrew is Abaddon, but in Greek he has the name Apollyon" (Rev. 9:11).

This king is the seventh and last king, the one that the false prophet empowers with authority to kill any that do not follow the beast of evil. Two more woes are to come.

John has been shown locusts that are like horses going into battle, with crowns of gold. Faces of men, hair of women, lion's teeth, breastplates of iron and wings that sound like chariots or running horses, along with stingers inflicting severe pain come to those who have taken the mark of the beast.

With the opening of the ninth chapter we see a star falling from heaven (Satan) and this connects to Revelation's twelfth chapter, with a third of the stars being cast down to earth as well as the dragon Leviathan. The angels were tested and a third were deceived, falling to Satan's deceit. The star is figurative and represents a literal living being, a person or king; one that was once revered and now fallen. Satan is this fallen angel and he holds the key to the bottomless pit. Are the locusts literal? I think it would be safe to say that these locusts are not the same that we know today. The fact continues, the world will not repent.

Fifth Bowl Poured

"Then the fifth angel poured out his bowl on the throne of the beast, and his kingdom became full of darkness; and they gnawed their tongues because of the pain. V11. They blasphemed the God of heaven because of their pains and their sores, and did not repent of their deeds" (Rev. 16:10–11).

Revelation, 2:13, Satan's throne was said to sit in the ancient city of Pergamum, Turkey, which was known for its idolatry and to where one of the seven churches resided. Eventually his kingdom becomes the world and this curse of darkness and pain will spread throughout.

The first bowl judgment also relates to men on earth that received the mark of the beast having a foul and loathsome sore, yet, nothing is mentioned of pain until the fifth bowl.

I feel extremely sorry for these souls chasing after this last evil beast. Because of the many generations before, ones that fell from truth, their descendants will be blinded to an allegiance of evil. Ultimately, they are eternally lost, haters of the true God. Their inheritance will be the earth, forever and ever, which eventually becomes a burned-out cinder.

Sixth Trumpet Blown

"Then the sixth angel sounded: And I heard a voice from the four horns of the golden altar which is before God, V14 saying to the sixth angel who had the trumpet, "Release the four angels who are bound at the great river Euphrates." V15 So the four angels, who had been prepared for the hour and day and month and year, were released to kill a third of mankind. V16 Now the number of the army of the horseman *was* two hundred million; I heard the number of them. V17 And thus I saw the horses in the vision: those who sat on them had breastplates of fiery red, hyacinth blue, and sulfur yellow; and the heads of the horses *were* like the heads of lions; and out of their mouths came fire, smoke, and brimstone. V18 By these three *plagues* a third of mankind was killed—by the fire and the smoke and the brimstone which came out of their mouths. V19 For their power is in their mouth and in their tails; for their tails *are* like serpents, having heads; and with them they do harm. V20

But the rest of mankind, who were not killed by these plagues, did not repent of the works of their hands, that they should not worship demons, and idols of gold, silver, brass, stone, and wood, which can neither see nor hear nor walk. V20 And they did not repent of their murders or their sorceries or their sexual immorality or their thefts" (Rev. 9:13–21).

The four angels who are bound at the great river Euphrates will be released to go out and cause the death of one third of mankind. Apostle John tells us he heard an exact numerical number of two hundred million. I believe this to be literal because he could have said that he heard an incalculable number, yet he gave a precise number. China could easily raise an army of that exact number, two hundred million! They have the manpower to fulfill the number that is prophesied.

"And the winepress was trampled outside the city, and blood came out of the winepress, up to the horse's bridles, for one thousand six hundred furlongs" (Rev. 14:20).

This informs us that the dead will extend a distance of an area of almost two hundred miles.

Why do we see horses and not mechanical vehicles, and are the horses real or symbolic?

"Then I saw an angel standing in the sun; and he cried with a loud voice, saying to all the birds that fly in the midst of heaven, "Come and gather together for the supper of the great God, V18 that you may eat the flesh of kings, the flesh of captains, the flesh of mighty men, the flesh of horses and of those who sit on them, and the flesh of all *people*, free and slave, both small and great" (Rev 19:17-18). "And the rest were killed with the sword which proceeded from the mouth of Him who sat upon the horse. And all the birds were filled with their flesh" (Rev. 19:21).

Some believe the horses are figurative and represent armored vehicles. Tanks and armored vehicles are not eaten by birds and as we see here the birds are eating the flesh of horses and the ones that ride them.

Interestingly, it is not only the sun that produces electromagnetic pulses, there is also a bomb that can completely neutralize anything that runs on electricity; this is called an E-bomb. It is not only the United States, many free nations fear this technology. One of these bombs could render a nation useless. This could be why the army of two hundred million use horses instead of mechanical vehicles. Could this be why the fifth head of Leviathan, the lion, has its great wings plucked? This bomb could render the mighty kingdom of the United States, represented by a lion, make it indefensible and bring it to its knees. We rely almost one hundred percent on electricity and this bomb would absolutely devastate this country; militarily and economically. Man would be cast back to the earliest of times. Most technology that we rely on would become useless. If modern technology couldn't do the job, horses could. The fourth bowl judgment suggest that the sun will eventually play an important part in causing the use of horses for warfare and is more than capable of drastically changing the way all militaries operate, especially if anything electronic is rendered useless.

Sixth Bowl Poured

"Then the sixth angel poured out his bowl on the great river Euphrates, and its water was dried up, so that the way of the kings from the east might be prepared. V13 And I saw three unclean spirits like frogs *coming* out of the mouth of the dragon, out of the mouth of the beast, and out of the mouth of the false prophet. V14 For they are spirits of demons, performing signs, *which* go out to the kings of the earth and of the whole world, to gather them to the battle of that great day of God Almighty. V15 "Behold, I am coming as a thief. Blessed *is* he who watches, and keeps his garments, lest he walk naked and they see his shame." V16 And they gathered them together to the place called in Hebrew, Armageddon" (Rev. 16:12–16).

At this time there will be Christians on earth surviving this hell, and verse 15 gives a blessing to those that "watch" and do not soil their garments. They will endure these hardships up to the return of our Lord and hold to the truth of God (1 Thess. 4:15).

The sixth angel pours out his bowl on the great river Euphrates and the river dries up and makes way for the kings from the East as they prepare for battle. John saw three unclean spirits like frogs coming out of the mouth of the dragon (Satan), out of the mouth of the beast (the evil kingdom of the world) and out of the mouth of the false prophet. These are spirits of demons performing signs as they go out to the kings of the world and gather them for that great day of battle. All nations will be gathered to come against Israel, at an event called Armageddon. The world will be in a frenzy, all caused by the ones that are not written in the Book of Life. Satan and his prophet cry out to the world that the Jews have caused their torment and Allah demands their deaths. These spirits will convince every nation to come against God's chosen people in every effort to destroy them. It will be the battle of the great day of God Almighty. The harvest of the grapes will then take place. The grapes represent the ones that have killed the saints and are considered lost, (Revelation 14) those that hate God. When the sixth trumpet and the sixth bowl are compared, we first see four angels that will have a direct influence in killing one third of mankind and are connected to an army of two hundred million.

What is so significant about the Euphrates River drying up so the kings from the East might be prepared? We now have tanks that can drive under water along with other amphibious vehicles that can drive on top of water. Bridges can be erected within hours. So why would this river hold back the world's largest army ever to march against mankind? I believe God gave us a sign, to warn those of biblical understanding to what is about to take place. Could the drying of the Euphrates be caused by scorching heat as foretold in the fourth bowl judgment? At this point I would also say the Lord is gathering his army to come against this evil force, for the time is short. Keep in mind that all nations come against Israel as told in the Book of Joel, Zechariah, Chapters 12 & 14 and Ezekiel, Chapter 38. China and other nations will be deceived by this evil kingdom, the false prophet and Satan the dragon. This can only be considered once the sixth trumpet and the sixth bowl are read together. At this date and time China is the likely candidate to raise the largest portion of this gigantic army of two hundred million, since it is east of the Euphrates River. The Book of Ezekiel does enlighten us that other armies will be drawn in to fight for the honor of the two kings. The three leopard heads (kingdoms) give dominance to the crowned leopard, representing the Middle East and China could be one of those kingdoms. Past wars will not compare to what is to come. Even after this great army of millions that partake in killing one third of the world's population will not repent for killing the prophets and saints or for any other sins they have committed. Russia will fully engage being the foundation of Satan's kingdom (Revelation 13:2). God will judge all nations as they gather in the Valley of Jehoshaphat. There will be one final battle before he reclaims the earth; all paths lead to Israel.

Seventh Trumpet Blown

"Then the seventh angel sounded: And there were loud voices in heaven, saying, "The kingdoms of this world have become *the kingdoms* of our Lord and of His Christ, and He shall reign forever and ever!' V16 And the twenty four elders who sat before God on their thrones fell on their faces and worshiped God, V17 saying: "We give You thanks O Lord God Almighty, The One who is and who was and who is to come, Because You have taken Your great power and reigned. V18 The nations were angry, and Your wrath has come, And the time of the dead, that they should be judged, And that You should reward Your servants the prophets and the saints, And those who fear Your name, small and great, And should destroy those who destroy the earth." V19 Then the temple of God was opened in heaven, and the ark of His covenant was seen in His temple. And there were lightnings, noises, thunderings, an earthquake, and great hail" (Rev. 11:15–19). This angel proclaims the kingdoms of the earth now belong to our Lord as the twenty four elders fall from their thrones to their faces, giving praise to God for his righteous judgment.

Where is the Ark of His Covenant? After the backsliding of Israel, God gave them a "certificate of divorce" and their temple was destroyed. I believe he removed the Ark and sent it back up to heaven which is later mentioned sitting in his temple while devastating events plague the earth. There will be lightning, noises, thundering and a great earthquake and the noise of hundred-pound hail stones as they pound the earth, diminishing life. Cities collapse and there is none to help. As it is written, if not for the intervention of God, even his elect would be lost.

Seventh Bowl Poured

"Then the seventh angel poured out his bowl into the air, and a loud voice came out of the temple of heaven, from the throne, saying, "It is done!" V18 And there were noises and thunderings and lightnings;

and there was a great earthquake, such a mighty and great earthquake as had not occurred since men were on the earth. 19 Now the great city was divided into three parts, and the cities of the nations fell. And great Babylon was remembered before God, to give her the cup of the wine of the fierceness of His wrath. V20 Then every island fled away, and the mountains were not found. V21 And great hail from heaven fell upon men, *each hailstone* about the weight of a talent. Men blasphemed God because of the plague of the hail, since that plague was exceedingly great" (Rev. 16:17–21). The pouring of the seventh bowl is different from the previous ones. The last is poured out into the air. Verse 19, Babylon, the great city connects to the first seal, the harlot, the great city. God has not forgotten this city, "MYSTERY BABYLON THE GREAT, THE MOTHER Of HARLOTS AND Of THE ABOMINATIONS OF THE EARTH." (Rev. 17:5). Ones of unlimited power and wealth that deceive the world. He has so much revulsion for what the city stood for that he strikes it again, not only by an earthquake but an earthquake with such destruction that since the time of man there has never been such a calamity. With such force the islands of the earth will disappear and literal mountains will be leveled as one hundred pound hail stones destroy the nations of the world. Our Father in heaven has now reclaimed the earth and the mystery of God is revealed to the world. Through the blood of his Son he has redeemed the world. For Jesus is the Lord of Lords.

The seventh trumpet and bowl judgment give a picture of a totally collapsed world. There are no longer mountains. All of their peaks have been lowered to ground level. A great earthquake, not since from the beginning of mankind, caused all this. Great hail will fall and the ones that survive are going through a hell on earth as few will survive this wrath. No wonder we are told that the meek shall inherit this planet. One day they will be removed to a new earth. Even with the end of God's mystery, man will still curse him. The world will eventually come to know the true God and his Son. The Lord will rule with an iron rod and all nations will come to Jerusalem and worship at the feet of the Jews, the twelve tribes, referring to Revelation 3:9. The end comes with God's perfect number, completeness, 777. Seven seals, seven trumpets and the seven bowls. There are those that claim there is no chronological order to the book of Revelation. As what has been presented, there is a complete order to this revelation.

Chapter 25

The Meek Shall Inherit the Earth

From the beginning, man would not listen to God and the end seems to repeat itself. As Satan is released from his prison mankind will once again become obstinate and chase after evil, believing in deceitful lies. It is unbelievable that after our Lord's thousand-year reign mankind will again fall into the hands of this deceiving spirit.

Isaiah 2:6 refers to the last days with the Jewish people taking up eastern ways and this does not help their position. Gentiles will also be caught up in the evil of this dark kingdom, caught in the clutches of Leviathan and drawn into the great war against Israel. Later, this sea beast will be destroyed by God as it attempts to flee Armageddon. These next verses say it all. No wonder the meek inherit the earth. Mankind, or what is left of them, along with the earth, will be completely shattered.

"Gather yourselves together, yes, gather together, O undesirable nation, V2 Before the decree is issued, Or the day passes like chaff, Before the Lord's fierce anger comes upon you, Before the day of the Lords anger comes upon you! V3 Seek the Lord, all you meek of earth, Who have upheld His Justice. Seek righteousness, seek humility. It may be that you will be hidden in the day of the Lord's anger" (Zeph. 2:1-3).

"Behold, the Lord makes the earth empty and makes it waste, Distorts its surface and scatters abroad its inhabitants" (Isa. 24:1).

"The earth is also defiled under its inhabitants, Because they have transgressed the laws, Changed the ordinance, Broken the everlasting covenant. V6 Therefore the curse has devoured the earth, And those who dwell in it are desolate. Therefore the inhabitants of the earth are burned, And few men are left" (Is. 24:5-6).

"Fear and the pit and the snare *Are* upon you, O inhabitant of the earth. V18 And it shall be *That* he who flees from the noise of the fear Shall fall into the pit, And he who comes up from the midst of the pit Shall be caught in the snare; For the windows from on high are open, And the foundations of the earth are shaken. V19 The earth is violently broken, The earth is split open, The earth is shaken exceedingly. V20 The earth shall reel to and fro like a drunkard, And shall totter like a hut; Its transgression shall be very heavy upon it, and it will fall, and not rise again. V21 It shall come to pass in that day *That* the Lord will punish on high the host of exalted ones, And on the earth the kings of the earth. V22 They will be gathered together, As prisoners are gathered in the pit, And will be shut up in the prison; After many days they will be punished. V23 Then the moon will be disgraced And the sun ashamed; For the Lord of hosts will reign On Mount Zion And in Jerusalem And before His elders, gloriously (Isa. 24:17-23).

"And it shall come to pass in that day," says the Lord God, "That I will make the sun go down at noon, And I will darken the earth in broad daylight; V10 I will turn your feasts into mourning, And all your songs into lamentation; I will bring sackcloth on every waist, And baldness on every head; I will make it like mourning an only *son*, And its end like a bitter day. V 11 "Behold, the days are coming," says the Lord God, "That I will send famine on the land, Not a famine of bread, Nor a thirst of water, But of hearing the words of the Lord. V12 They shall wander from sea to sea, And from north to east; they shall run to and fro, seeking the word of the Lord, But shall not find *it* (Amos 8:9-12).

"But the day of the lord will come as a thief in the night, in which the heavens will pass away with a great noise, and the elements will melt with fervent heat; both the earth and the works that are in it will be burned up. V11 Therefore, since all these things will be dissolved, what manner *of persons* ought you to be in holy conduct and godliness, V12 looking for and hastening the coming of the day of God, because of which the heavens will be dissolved, being on fire, and the elements will melt with fervent heat? V13 Nevertheless we, according to His promise, look for new heavens and a new earth in which righteousness dwells" (2 Peter 3:10-13). This takes place after the Lord's thousand year reign.

"Heaven and earth will pass away, but My words will by no means pass away" (Matt. 24:35).

"Then the moon will be disgraced And the sun ashamed" (Isa. 24:23). The life-giving light that has been given by these two objects that were created at the beginning of this world now despise the earth because of what it has become.

Chapter 26

A Panoramic View

How do we draw the whole picture together? The metaphor of Leviathan not only begins with the Book of Job, and also with Revelation's twelfth chapter. Leviathan's tail swept the heavens and with its evil persuaded a third of heaven's angels to come to earth, along with another evil entity, Satan. Their minds were not set on holy things but rather a lust for strange earthly flesh. They willfully selected wives and later produced off-spring of great evil. The spirit of man and angel were not to mix; this was not in God's plan. Wickedness consumed the earth as war broke out in heaven. Evil followed Satan and his angels to earth and here they will stay and our Lord will give to them what they deserve. God's judgment was harsh as the story of Noah now enters. The earth reels in a flood, destroying all life with an exception of eight faithful beings. Earth then repopulates as Satan roamed the planet as a hungry lion, turning whatever he touched into evil. Our Father in heaven knew mankind could not stand against this being of beauty and magnificent power, so our Lord Jesus became manifest through the flesh of man. He was sent to teach the world how to combat Satan and his followers. Because of the hate for truth, Jesus lived a short life. The world put him to the cross and continued to resist God's message as war, death, pestilence and pain continued. As God declared; from the beginning man would not listen.

Today we see signs of an increase in martyrdom because of the name of Jesus, which leads us to Matthew 24:9. There is an increase in wars, famines, pestilence and earthquakes. Just a few years back it was shown that there was no increase in earthquakes, but recently stronger quakes have increased in number and intensity. The news media is becoming increasingly fascinating as it parallels prophecy that has been written more than two thousand years ago. Fear and doubt are beginning to rise, as terrorism is being broadcast throughout the world. Reality has now set in. Many in the West are seeing a possibility of losing this war on freedom, falling to a religion of extreme intolerance.

Israel's survival depends on the United States as this nation intends to make Jerusalem their capitol. Wall Street has surged beyond reason and I fully believe the world will continue to marvel at this great city that controls world trade, as did the apostle John. One day Israel will sign a seven-year peace treaty with its opposition, which will eventually fulfill God's four hundred and ninety year curse on the Jew. In the middle of the treaty, Israel will be attacked and will fall. In this same time frame there is a good possibility that the great trade city, Mystery Babylon that reigns over all kings and kingdoms, at her pinnacle of power will suddenly come to an end, all with the help of Leviathan's ten horns. New York City will be consumed in a ball of fire, ushering in the apocalypse.

As prophesied, at the very end of the Israel's existence it will come under the rule of the Gentile and there will be no one to help. This tiny speck of land will once again be invaded. If not killed, their men, women and children will be sold as slaves and relocated to other lands until the determined forty-two months are fulfilled. All nations will hunt down the Christian and Jew and the ones of evil will honor a god of war, the one that will remove the word of truth. The earth will be of one mind and of one faith, all believing in unity and all bowing to Allah. Throughout history, there has never been a time that the entire globe accepts a one world religion. Islam will try to fulfill Satan's ambition; exterminate all Christians and Jews, especially the Jew.

Armageddon is a place to where all nations will deliver their armies, and there the true God of the Hebrews will send his Son and his army to consume the evil ones with fire. Every nation that comes against Israel will be destroyed and all nations are involved. For forty-two months the rule of evil will prevail, grinding the world to its knees until God's court is seated and judgment falls in favor of the saints. Jesus will eventually rule with his martyrs for a thousand years and then he will turn his authority back to his Father as he becomes all in all. Leviathan will fall and Satan's time will end in a lake of fire. God's glory will overwhelm death. For those who overcome, their tears will dry up and no longer will there be any memory of this planet.

God's Promise

In the very last years, just before the return of our Lord, I believe Israel will become the center of the earth. Everything will revolve around her. Many claim that God will have nothing to do with this small nation because of backsliding, breaking his covenant. Abraham, Isaac and Jacob were given, by God, the land of Israel, a promise that they would inherit for a thousand generations. What happened? Israel faltered as they fell to other gods. Yet, God did not completely remove his hand from them. At the very end of Revelation; his promise will endure and the world will come to Israel and praise God. He will not do this because of what the later generations have done, but for what he swore to their forefathers because of his name's sake, Lev. 26: 38-46, Deut. 1:8-11, 6:10-25, 7:6-10, 31:6-8, 1 Sam. 12:22-25, Jer. 14:20-22, Ezek. 36:16-38. All paths lead to Israel, especially God's beloved city, Jerusalam, as described in Revelation's last two chapters.

Chapter 27

The Author's Last Thoughts

"Those by the wayside are the ones who hear; then the devil comes and takes away the word out of their hearts, lest they should believe and be saved" (Luke 8:12). This verse relates to this book or to the ones that are considered "tumble weeds." The faithful can lose what they have attained if they do not adhere to biblical instruction or not retaining scripture, which can lead to ones downfall. Be aware: Satan will do his very best to work with you, and if there is an interest in working with him, you will lose.

Throughout this book I have pointed to Islam as the religion that Satan will eventually use to destroy Judaism and Christianity. My mission is to lead you to an awareness and not hatred. Many believe the apocalypse will begin within this decade, this is why I believe Islam is the religion that Satan will use to deceive the world. As I have stated: there are a tremendous amount of loving and great people of the Islamic faith. Do not turn your back on them. Pray for them as you pray for your brother. If you claim to be Christian, understand your God and adhere to scripture. Open your Bible and study; hopefully it will help you endure to the end.

With a new president now in office the stock market is zooming out of sight. Along with this, the U.S. government is becoming more vocal. If there are no intensions to help control rogue nations, the WTO will move their trade to other countries. This is how powerful this organization is. A lack of trade can be devastating, especially to a nation like China. There are countries that have not fared well and have been defiant against an organized world trade system. New York City, along with the WTO is conquering the world.

With its superior technology, America has lived under an umbrella of impregnable safety. In 2001, with the destruction of the World Trade Buildings, that comfort evaporated. Since then we have boasted that the mightiest army in the world would annihilate terrorism and bring the matter to a close. The Taliban are stronger now and more numerous than at the beginning of the U.S. involvement in Afghanistan. Terrorism has spread like cancer as it continues to surge. Several years ago, many fractions of extreme Islam did not exist, such as ISIS.

This last decade has proven to the world, that Satan's influence cannot be stopped. Revelation's 13:2 is becoming enlightened to the fact that the leopard's spots are beginning to dominate the world. Germany and many other countries continue their path of immigration; dooming their future. In a few short years the Islamic population will dominate their nation, directing how they will live and what kind of law they will serve under. Many Europeans believe it is good that there is an influx of Middle Eastern people; the more the merrier. One day matters will fall in place, all with the rise of a very influential prophet. Islam will bow and unite as this prophesied man of faith creates miracles. After this, the world will be prepared to receive the seventh and last king, Satan.

As prophesied, Russia is now involved in the Middle East and their technology is becoming troublesome. President Vladimir Putin has once again been voted in to rule over his nation. His eyes are defiant as he glares at the United States since economic sanctions began to grow against Russia. Most European nations have now joined in and back the U.S. for coming against Russian aggression taking place in England, poisoning one of their own, an ex-spy and his daughter. Putin blasted the U.S. for directing the economic attack and promised that there would be retaliation as he also boasted that they have acquired a new technology, a new missile and that there is no defense against it. We shrug it off as propaganda; is it? A short time later he commented that if the U.S. attacked Syria, this would start World War 3. Well, that just happened.

Turkey and Egypt are showing signs of breaking tradition with the U.S. as they continue to buddy up to the bear. As usual, America continues to play the harlot, climbing in bed with any that gives her pleasure. So far, China has stayed neutral and this is because of trade. This could possibly continue until the harlot's demise.

A vast majority of Christians, especially in this modern era, do not want to face the reality that God would put his faithful, including their children and grandchildren through a tribulation that cannot be compared to any other. No one can change these prophesied events, but prayer and evangelizing could save thousands, if not millions from the roaming lion that will try to devour them. Inform others on the matter of Leviathan so they just might understand the God they worship and that he will eventually destroy this great city that deceives the world.

Many people question me about the end days. When I explain what we are about to face, some actually look as though they are about to faint and then the conversation ends. If Christians have enough faith and knowledge of the last book of the Bible, that will then prepare them to face this frightening metaphor of Leviathan. They are the ones that will endure to the end; this is the blessing! To hold back your loved ones from the truth of Revelation could very easily condemn their souls for an eternity.

Daniel was informed (Dan. 12:11-12) that at the time when the daily sacrifice is taken away and the "abomination of desolation" stands in the temple of God and proclaims himself as God, this will begin Satan's wrath, which will last 1290 days. I believe this points to the seventh and last bowl as severe judgment comes upon mankind. Verse 12, describe the ones that endure the last 45 days, which bring us to 1335 days, are called "blessed." At this time of the end, the world will curse the God of heaven because of the one hundred pound hail stones destroying and killing many (Job 38:22-23). Great lightning and thunderings will shake the souls of men. New York City will be remembered by God as he strikes it with the greatest of earthquakes. Islands disappear and mountains are brought down to ground level as God reclaims the earth. Our mission is to hold on to what you gained spiritually and do not curse

God when this takes place, endure!

With the accumulation of scripture, a metamorphosis is seen in Leviathan. From Job's scaly fire breathing dragon to a sea serpent with seven heads and ten horns, to the understanding that this metaphor is representing kings and kingdoms; power, pride and evil.

Is there an urgency to call believers out of New York City, the great city? Absolutely! The need to understand God's word is an understatement. I have seen interviews with people living in New York City and the majority do not believe one thing will happen to them. You would think the destruction of the World Trade Buildings would resonate through their minds forever. It is as if this event never took place. God declares he will try to call his saints out of the city before it is destroyed. Anyone living in New York City or within its vicinity might consider moving far from this location; especially within the next several years.

Two prophecies are about to collide. The gospel of the Lord is about to be given to all dialects and a great city is about to reign over all kings and kingdoms and then the end begins.

Without a doubt, the second head of Leviathan (Persia) is breathing and its prophet will arrive shortly. After this, the beast's horns will rise and then Satan will begin to smile.

The Coming Glory

In the Book of Joel, the second chapter describes a great army, a great strong people, the likes that has never been seen before, or will ever be seen again. This can only be compared to the great tribulation. After this event ends, God will again pour his spirit out on all flesh and then your sons and daughters shall prophesy, (Joel 2:28). The pouring out of God's spirit takes place only after the most horrifying event that comes upon mankind.

At the very end, after the great tribulation, events will take place that will leave the world in awe. Revelation's Chapter 21, begins with apostle John now seeing a new heaven and a new earth, for the first earth had passed away. There is no more sea with the passing away of the earth The "sea" could represent the roaring of the sea, describing the stress that comes upon the nations in the very last of days. This could also indicate that there is no place for Leviathan to hide, for the reptile in the sea has been slain by God in the great battle of Armageddon! John then sees a great holy city descending from heaven and was named the "New Jerusalem." In verse 3, John then heard a voice from heaven, "Behold, the tabernacle of God *is* with men, and He will dwell with them, and they shall be His people. God Himself will be with them *and be* their God." John continues and informs us that all tears will be wiped away as there will be no more death, sorrow, crying or pain. Our former lives are gone. We are to be given a new body and mind. There will be no more memory of this earth. In verse 5, God declares that all things are to be made new. God then declares "It is done" and that he is the Alpha and the Omega, the beginning and the end and he who overcomes will inherit all things.

John is about to be shown a city that is so awesome, so dreamlike, I don't know if words would be able to fully describe this place. John 14:1-4, Jesus explained to believers "I go to prepare a place for you." "I will come again and receive you to Myself." John is now seeing what Jesus promised; a place for us!

In Rev. 21:9, the angel now shows John "the bride, the Lambs wife." In Spirit the angel brings John to a great high mountain so that he could see the entire holy New Jerusalem that was descending out of heaven from God. The light of God radiated from it, "like a most precious stone." The city had twelve gates and each was described as a pearl. Three gates were on each side of the cities walls and inscribed on the gates were the names of the twelve tribes, the children of Israel. The city was supported by twelve foundations with the names of the twelve apostles. The foundation of its wall was covered with many precious stones. It was expressed that the city was in the shape of a cube. Its length, width and height are the same and measured 12,000 furlongs, approximately 1500 miles. It was written that to walk across the city of Nineveh took three days. The New Jerusalem would dwarf this city.

John did not see a temple inside the city, but he knew that God and Jesus, from thereon in, would be his temple. There is no need for the sun or the moon to illuminate the city, as Jesus is its light! The nations that are saved walk in its light as the kings of nations bring glory and honor to God Almighty into the city. The gates will constantly stay open, for there is no night. Only those written in the Lamb's Book of Life will enter. John was then shown a river, a river of water of life that was crystal clear proceeding from the throne of God and of the Lamb. In the middle of the street, on both sides of the river, he saw a tree of life which every month, each tree yielded twelve fruits. The tree's leaves were for healing the nations. The 490 year curse has now been removed. God and Jesus shall sit on their thrones and his servants shall serve God. Those that are in the city that have God's name on their foreheads, shall gaze upon the face of this magnificent creator, of this endless universe. No man has ever seen the face of God.

"Indeed I will make *those* of the synagogue of Satan, who say they are Jews and are not, but lie—indeed I will make them come and worship before your feet, and to know that I have loved you" (Rev. 3:9).

"He who overcomes, I will make him a pillar in the temple of My God, and he shall go out no more. I will write on him the name of My God, and the name of the city of My God, the New Jerusalem, which comes down out of heaven from My God. And *I will write* on *him* My new name" (Rev. 3:12).

R. L. Nelson

Bibliography

Andrews, Edmund L., *Greenspan Warns Congress Not to Create Trade Barriers* - The New York Times, March 12, 2004.

Arnold, Jack l, *Church History, The Fall of Rome, Early Church History, part 16, IIIM Magazine Online, Volume 1, Number 30, September 20-26, 1999.*

Baer, Robert, *Sleeping With the Devil, 2003*

Beason, Doug, PhD, *The E-Bomb*, 2005.

Byers, Marvin, *Yasser Arafat: An Apocalyptic Character,* 1996.

Canter, Ergun Mehmet, & Emir Fethi Canter, *Unveiling Islam, 2002.*

Catholic Encyclopedia, *Illuminati*, New Advent, 2009.

Cuddy, Dennis Laurence, PH.D, *Secret Records Revealed,* 1999, *The Globalists*, 2001.

Curtis & Tallis, *Forgotten Empire: The World of Ancient Persia*, 2005.

Davidson, Ben, SpaceWeatherNews.com, effects of the sun.

Frye, Richard N, *The Heritage of Persia*, 1963.

Gibbon, Edward, *Gibbon's Decline and fall of the Roman Empire,* 1995.

Greenhaven Press, *Islam, Opposing Viewpoints,* 2004.

Kadivar, Cyrus, *We Are Awake*, The Iranian, Jan. 25, 2002.

Hobbs, Thomas, *Leviathan*, 1651.

Rosenthal, Marvin, *The Pre-Wrath Rapture of the Church*, 1990.

Schifrin, Nick, *Pakistan Expands Taliban Offensive*, ABC News, May 6, 2009.

Spurlock, Morgan, *30 Days "Muslims and America,"* reality television program, 2005.

Stiglitz, Joseph E, Globalization and its Discontents, 2002.

Wiesehofer, Josef, *Ancient Persia,* 1996, 2001.

Yusufali, Abdullah, *Roman Transliteration of the Holy Qur'an,* 1978

Web resources

www.bneimenashe.com, a lost tribe of Israel Web site.

www.clintonlibrary.gov, NAFTA.

www.g7.utoronto.ca, Web for G7 & G8.

www.icj-cij.org, International Court Of Justice (World Court).

www.jeanmonnetprogram.org, The NAFTA in the WTO System.

www. islamreligion.com

www.militantislammonitor.org, the Militant Islam Monitor Web site

www.newswithviews.com

www.pewforum.org, the Pew Forum web site gives a status of religions.

www.silencingchristians.com.

www.wtca.com, World Trade Centers Association.

www.wto.org, the World Trade Organization Web site.

www.wycliffe.org

Index